UNIVERSITY OF NORTH CAROLINA AT CHAPEL HILL
DEPARTMENT OF ROMANCE LANGUAGES

NORTH CAROLINA STUDIES
IN THE ROMANCE LANGUAGES AND LITERATURES

Founder: URBAN TIGNER HOLMES
Editor: STIRLING HAIG

Distributed by:

UNIVERSITY OF NORTH CAROLINA PRESS
CHAPEL HILL
North Carolina 27514
U.S.A.

NORTH CAROLINA STUDIES IN THE
ROMANCE LANGUAGES AND LITERATURES
Number 224

THE STATUS OF THE READING SUBJECT
IN THE *LIBRO DE BUEN AMOR*

THE STATUS OF THE READING SUBJECT IN THE *LIBRO DE BUEN AMOR*

BY
MARINA SCORDILIS BROWNLEE

CHAPEL HILL

NORTH CAROLINA STUDIES IN THE ROMANCE
LANGUAGES AND LITERATURES
U.N.C. DEPARTMENT OF ROMANCE LANGUAGES

1985

Library of Congress Cataloging in Publication Data

Brownlee, Marina Scordilis.
   The status of the reading subject in the Libro de buen amor.

   (North Carolina studies in the Romance languages and literatures; 224)
   Bibliography: p.
   1. Ruiz, Juan, fl. 1343. Libro de buen amor. 2. Reader-response criticism.
I. Title. II. Series.

PQ6430.B7 1985   861'.1   85-2903

© 1985 Department of Romance Languages, The University of North Carolina at Chapel Hill.

I.S.B.N. 0-8078-9228-9

DEPÓSITO LEGAL: V. 550 - 1985   I.S.B.N. 84-599-0534-9
ARTES GRÁFICAS SOLER, S. A. - LA OLIVERETA, 28 - 46018 VALENCIA - 1985

ACKNOWLEDGEMENTS

I wish to acknowledge the help of a few people to whom I am indebted.

R. S. Willis introduced me to the *Libro de buen amor* at Princeton and made the study of its manifold complexities an exciting endeavor. Karl D. Uitti's seminars on Old French literature have influenced my reading of medieval Spanish literature.

Samuel G. Armistead and Alan D. Deyermond I thank for their careful reading and valuable criticism of my work in general and this manuscript in particular.

Stephen G. Nichols has made medieval literary studies at Dartmouth a dynamic enterprise. I am grateful for his guidance and encouragement.

Finally, I thank the National Endowment for the Humanities for a fellowship which enabled me to research and write this book, and Dartmouth College for subventing its publication.

To K. B.

TABLE OF CONTENTS

	Page
CHAPTER	
I. CRITICAL PERSPECTIVES	11
II. THE PROSE PROLOGUE AND THE AUGUSTINIAN PARADOX	23
III. TWO FIGURAL READINGS	36
IV. THE NARRATOR/PROTAGONIST/AUTHOR CONFIGURATION	59
V. PARABLES OF INTERPRETATION	74
VI. MISAPPROPRIATED *Exempla*	88
VII. THE CIRCULARITY OF STABLE IRONY	98
VIII. GENRE AS MEANING	111
IX. CONCLUSION: JUAN RUIZ AND THE *Mester de Clerecía*	122
BIBLIOGRAPHY	131
INDEX	137

I. CRITICAL PERSPECTIVES

The status of the reading subject — formerly considered unproblematic and ungenerative — is now the focus of intense critical attention. This foregrounding of the reader's role stems from the recognition that a literary text is not a static artifact which is passively received by its readers. Rather, it represents a dynamic process whereby a given reader functions as mediator between text and author. As a result, reader-oriented criticism makes accessible previously inaccessible dimensions of the text. For as Wolfgang Iser explains in *The Act of Reading*, "the traditional form of interpretation, based on the search for a single meaning, set out to *instruct* the reader, consequently, it tended to ignore both the character of the text as a happening and the experience of the reader that is activated by this happening." [1]

While reader-oriented studies of modern literature abound, few have as yet been undertaken in the context of medieval Spanish literature. Moreover, the optic of reading theory is particularly relevant to a study of the *Libro de buen amor* (= *Libro*) by the Archpriest of Hita, Juan Ruiz — the undisputed masterpiece of fourteenth-century Spain. Referred to as the "Spanish Boccaccio," the Archpriest produces a text which overtly acknowledges the paramount importance of the reading subject. For in stanza 70 the author, in effect, disappears from his text — in order to impose the primacy of the text itself and, therefore, of the reader's crucial interpretive role:

---

[1] Wolfgang Iser, *The Act of Reading. A Theory of Aesthetic Response* (Baltimore: The Johns Hopkins University Press, 1978). p. 22.

> De todos instrumentes yo, libro, só pariente:
> bien o mal, quál puntares, tal diré, ciertamente;
> quál tú dezir quesieres, y faz punto e tente;
> si puntarme sopieres siempre me abrás en miente. [2]
>
> [I, this book, am akin to all instruments of music: according as you point (play music) well or badly, so, most assuredly, will I speak; in whatever way you choose to speak, make a point (stop) there and hold fast; if you know how to point me (pluck my strings), you will always hold me in mind. (28)]

The reader-oriented perspective voiced in stanza 70 serves as an opening signal for what amounts to a thematization of the problem of interpretation, which I maintain, is the work's principal theme. Juan Ruiz constructs an intentionally polysemous text whereby he repeatedly calls upon his audience to engage in interpretive reading.

Indeed, the foregrounding of the reader's participation in a given text is potentially as constructive an interpretive tool as the study of genre has proven to be. In this regard Walter Ong observes that: "just as each genre grows out of what went before, so each new role that readers are made to assume is related to previous roles." [3]

Ong's observation concerning the historicity and evolutionary nature of readership (of the role into which the reader is cast by the author) is of special importance to the *Libro* for several interrelated reasons. Firstly, the Archpriest explicitly addresses himself to many diverse types of inscribed readers throughout his work. [4] In and of itself this procedure is an intriguing and somewhat unexpected phenomenon within the context of fourteenth-century Spanish poetry (given the norms of audience in the *mester de clerecía*

---

[2] Raymond S. Willis, ed. and trans., *Libro de buen amor* (Princeton: Princeton University Press, 1972), p. 29. Willis bases his edition on MS *G* wherever possible, with recourse to MSS *S* and *T* when necessary. (See his pp. liii ff.) I rely on this edition unless otherwise indicated.

[3] Walter J. Ong, "The Writer's Audience is Always a Fiction," *PMLA*, 90 (1975), 12.

[4] The inscribed reader is quite simply, the reader or readers who are explicitly identified within the text. See in this connection Diego Catalán, with Suzy Petersen, "'Aunque omne non goste la pera del peral...' (Sobre la 'sentencia' de Juan Ruiz y la de su *buen amor*)," *Hispanic Review*, 38, 5 (1970), esp. pp. 78-82.

corpus, upon whose poetic practices the Archpriest bases himself in large measure). [5] However, the role of the inscribed reader takes on a vital importance when viewed as system, since it is only at that point that we may discern the nature of the implied reader (and implied author) of the work as a whole. [6]

The exercise of reconstructing the implied reader, beyond its integral value for interpretation of the *Libro,* has significant implications for the function of genre therein as well. For clearly, the function of the reader is determined by the generic affiliation(s) with which an author endows his particular text. (As Hans-Robert Jauss has meaningfully remarked, "la littérature médiévale romane n'est pas simplement une somme arbitraire, mais un ordre latent ou une suite d'ordres de genres littéraires.") [7] By extension then, the study of genre itself sheds light on the overall structure of the text, hence of its meaning. These two types of literary investigation are mutually illuminating.

Reception of the *Libro* — its history of interpretation — has been (and continues to be) widely divergent. The *Corbacho* (1438) of the Archpriest of Talavera refers to Juan Ruiz's text twice, both times as a *tractado,* a morally edifying treatise. [8] By contrast, another contemporary opinion (that of the Marqués de Santillana in his epistolary disquisition on literary history written to the Constable of Portugal [1445-49]), speaks of the *Libro* primarily in formally didactic terms, as a poetically innovative work. [9] Yet

---

[5] See G. B. Gybbon-Monypenny, "The Spanish *Mester de Clerecía* and Its Intended Public: Concerning the Validity as Evidence of Passages of Direct Address to the Audience," *Medieval Miscellany Presented to Eugène Vinaver,* eds., Brian Dutton, J. W. Haskell and John E. Keller (Manchester: Manchester University Press, 1965), pp. 230-44. See in addition John K. Walsh, "Juan Ruiz and the *mester de clerecía:* Lost Context and Lost Parody in the *Libro de buen amor,*" *Romance Philology,* 33 (1979), 62-86.

[6] "The concept of the implied reader designates a network of response-inviting structures, which impel the reader to grasp the text. No matter who or what he may be, the real reader is always offered a particular role to play, and it is this role that constitutes the concept of the implied reader" (Iser, *The Act of Reading,* pp. 34-35).

[7] Hans-Robert Jauss, "Littérature médiévale et théorie des genres," *Poétique,* 1 (1970), 91.

[8] Joaquín González Muela, ed., *Arcipreste de Talavera o Corbacho* (Madrid: Castalia, 1970), pp. 54, 195.

[9] Manuel Durán, ed., *Poesías completas del Marqués de Santillana,* II (Madrid: Castalia, 1980), p. 218.

another — appreciably different — attitude towards the *Libro* (culled from sixteenth-century manuscript evidence) indicates that it was perceived and exploited by some as a *cancionero*, a compendium of poetic fragments which could serve as a valuable source of entertainment for a minstrel's performance.[10]

More than five centuries after its composition, the meaning produced by the *Libro* continues to perplex, even elude, its readers. For the same three divergent attitudes indicated above from the fifteenth- and sixteenth-century interpreters (three largely contradictory interpretations) prevail today, with some modifications.

The detailed researching of the text carried out by Félix Lecoy in 1938 led him to interpret it primarily as an *ars amatoria* with a bi-partite structure:

> A qui lit de bout en bout le *Libro de buen amor,* sans idée préconçue, il apparaît immédiatement que l'essentiel de l'ouvrage est constitué par deux corps de récits indépendants, mais qui présentent, chacun de leur côté, une unité de conception et de développement bien marquée.[11]

The two central episodes which Lecoy identifies are that of Doña Endrina (sts. 653-891) and the battle between Lady Lent and Lord Meatseason (sts. 1067-1314). The outcome of this second episode (and of the poem as a whole), according to Lecoy, is to "chanter le retour de la joie après la période de tristesse et de mortification du carême, et . . . il s'élève jusqu'à une glorification enthousiaste du printemps, de l'amour et de la vie" (p. 352).

Around the fundamentally bi-partite division of the *Libro* Lecoy groups several episodes into a kind of "satellite" function, intended to reinforce his view of the work as a whole as an art of love.

---

[10] See Lucius G. Moffatt, "The Evidence of Early Mentions of the Archpriest of Hita or of His Work," *MLN*, 75 (1960), 33-40, esp. 39-40. See also Samuel G. Armistead, "An Unnoticed Fifteenth-Century Citation of the *Libro de buen amor*," *Hispanic Review*, 41 (1973), 88-91; and Mary-Anne Vetterling, "The Rediscovery of the *Libro de buen amor*," *Dieciocho*, 4 (1981), 24-33.

[11] Félix Lecoy, *Recherches sur le 'Libro de buen amor' de Juan Ruiz.* Reprinted with a new Prologue, supplementary Bibliography and Index by A. D. Deyermond (Farnborough, Hants: Gregg International, 1974), p. 352.

This same basic structural division has been retained more recently by Roger M. Walker and Oliver T. Myers.[12] Starting from Lecoy's structural conception, however, they proceed to derive an interpretation of the *Libro* which seriously contradicts his. For Walker and Myers alike the *Libro* is a profoundly moralizing work in which the second part reverses the meaning generated by the first. In Myers's words: "the didactic message of Part I is that love is inseparable from life and stems unavoidably from our very existence. Part II teaches that love leads inevitably to death, and that there is no hope of lasting love on earth except for the love of God" (p. 84).

In a cogent analysis of the three basic critical traditions of *Libro* scholarship,[13] Colbert Nepaulsingh lucidly presents the evidence offered by Lecoy and his successors, at the same time pointing to the limitations of each of their theories. Nepaulsingh quite rightly reminds us of the inherent danger of structural oversimplification in dealing with Juan Ruiz: "The major problem with the structure of all the episodes of the book, satellite as well as central, is their shifting perspective: at times their tone seems didactic and sincere and at others it is blatantly sinful and ironic."[14]

This relentless shift in perspective leads M. K. Read[15] and Cesáreo Bandera[16] to interpret the *Libro* as a calculated illustration of the "crisis of language" in the fourteenth century. On the other hand, Anthony Zahareas has recently posited the defining sociohistorical context of the *Libro* as that of the "fourteenth-century crisis of celibacy."[17] In response to this same modulation between

---

[12] Roger M. Walker, "Towards an Interpretation of the *Libro de buen amor*," *Bulletin of Hispanic Studies*, 43 (1966), 1-10; Oliver T. Myers, "Symmetry of Form in the *Libro de buen amor*," *Philological Quarterly*, 51 (1972), 74-84.

[13] The Lecoy school, the Spitzer school and the Castro/Lida de Malkiel school.

[14] Colbert Nepaulsingh, "The Structure of the *Libro de buen amor*," *Neophilologus*, 61 (1977), 59.

[15] M. K. Read, "Man Against Language: A Linguistic Perspective on the Theme of Alienation in the *Libro de buen amor*," *MLN*, 96 (1981), 237-60.

[16] Cesáreo Bandera, "De la apertura del *Libro* de Juan Ruiz a Derrida y viceversa," *Dispositio*, 2 (1977), 54-66.

[17] Anthony N. Zahareas, "Structure and Ideology in the *Libro de buen amor*," *La Corónica*, 7 (1977), 92-104.

serious and humorous registers, Menéndez Pidal concludes that the work is essentially a comical deflation of medieval didacticism. The *Libro* is not, for him, "un libro didáctico en serio; es un brote muy tardío... la despedida humorística a la época didáctica de la literatura medieval." [18] He further defines the *Libro* as "un vasto Cancionero, engastado en una biografía humorística" (p. 211). Recalling Menéndez Pidal's judgment, Leo Sptizer changes its emphasis, emending the earlier definition by ascribing to it a decidedly didactic framework: "yo recalcaría especialmente el término 'humorística,' con lo que lo biográfico pasa a segundo término y se reduce a la categoría de recurso técnico [19] ... Yo definiría el *Libro de buen amor* 'un vasto Cancionero engastado en una autobiografía humorística, que se engasta en un tratado ascético-moral.' " [20]

Once again recognizing the problematic nature of the *Libro* which is generated precisely from its shifting perspectives, Américo Castro and María Rosa Lida de Malkiel (who represent the third major school of criticism) situate it generically in terms of Arabic and Hebraic models of autobiographical literature respectively. Lida categorically rejects Lecoy's schema, affirming that:

> La forma cerrada, con acción central y andadura dinámica que Lecoy ... recorta en el *Libro* falsea incurablemente lo que Juan Ruiz de hecho escribió. No hay una primera parte (coplas 71-909) que desarrolle el aprendizaje amoroso, ya que el único triunfo es el de Don Melón, no del protagonista en primera persona, y al reaparecer éste reaparecen los fracasos, y no hay una segunda parte (950-1043), fiel al ritmo de la liturgia y de las estaciones, ya

---

[18] Ramón Menéndez Pidal, *Poesía juglaresca y orígenes de las literaturas románicas*, 6th ed. (Madrid: Instituto de Estudios Políticos, 1957), p. 209. In this context, John K. Walsh avers that: "A persistent reference to the works cast in *quaderna vía* may not be the root joke, the sustaining parody, or the dark secret of all residual ambiguities. But it was the likeliest start for Juan Ruiz's initial caprice, and may be the safest clue in our distant restoration of that whim." ("Juan Ruiz and the *Mester de Clerecía*," p. 86.)

[19] Leo Spitzer, "En torno al arte del Arcipreste de Hita," *Lingüística e historia literaria* (Madrid: Gredos, 1955), p. 138.

[20] Spitzer, "En torno al arte del Arcipreste," p. 142. Acknowledging a debt to Spitzer, but departing from Spitzer's view substantially, Anthony N. Zahareas advances the thesis that: "the persona in the *Libro* is created for ironic situations and that it is more conspicuous as an artistic creation than as a didactic necessity" (*The Art of Juan Ruiz Archpriest of Hita* [Madrid: Estudios de Literatura Española, 1965], p. 11.)

que las alusiones al calendario se limitan a las coplas 1067-1321, esto es a menos de la mitad. [21]

Focusing on the narrator's role, Castro finds evidence for arguing that Ibn Hazm's *risala, The Dove's Neckring,* is Juan Ruiz's model, while María Rosa Lida de Malkiel finds greater affinities between the Hispano-Hebraic *maqamat*, specifically, *The Book of Delights,* and the *Libro.* [22]

While the present reader-oriented study of the *Libro* finds the search for an autobiographical paradigm to be substantially more fruitful than Lecoy's interpretation (which fails to account for many textual problems), it also sees the Archpriest's text as being rooted primarily in Christian literary tradition as will become apparent in the pages to follow. (This perspective, of course, does not deny the potential importance of the *Libro*'s use of Semitic models.)

Finally, there has emerged of late a new school of *crítica ruiziana* which stems from the autobiographical approach of Lida de Malkiel and Castro. In contradistinction to their findings, however, this new vein of critical investigation seeks to interpret the *Libro* as a coherent whole in terms of hagiography. Chief among this group of critics are Colbert Nepaulsingh and André Michalski. Nepaulsingh suggestively discusses the *Libro* as an inversion of the constructs and values traditionally associated with the genre of saint's life. He speaks of the Archpriest's poem as an *imitatio Daemonii* (rather than an *imitatio Christi*), as *exemplum ex negativo.* [23] In another thoughtful study, Michalski sees the *Libro* also in terms of hagiographic parody — but analyzing it specifically as a parodic inversion of St. Augustine's *Confessions,* as an "anti-Augustine." [24]

---

[21] María Rosa Lida de Malkiel, "Nuevas notas para la interpretación del *Libro de buen amor*," *Nueva Revista de Filología Hispánica,* 13 (1959), 19.

[22] See María Rosa Lida de Malkiel, *Two Spanish Masterpieces: The 'Book of Good Love' and 'The Celestina*.*"* Illinois Studies in Language and Literature, 49 (Urbana: University of Illinois Press, 1961), 10-11, 20-25; and Américo Castro, "El *Libro de buen amor* del Arcipreste de Hita," *Comparative Literature,* 4 (1952), 193-213.

[23] "Structure," pp. 64-73. See also Lida, *Two Spanish Masterpieces,* pp. 29-30.

[24] André Michalski, "La parodia hagiográfica y el dualismo eros-thanatos en el *Libro de buen amor*," *Actas del I Congreso Internacional sobre el Arcipreste de Hita,* ed., Manuel Criado de Val (Barcelona: S.E.R.E.S.A., 1973), p. 77.

Like genre-theories and reader-roles, which Ong correctly perceives as being evolutionary (rather than revolutionary) in nature, such is also the case, to a considerable extent, with a given corpus of literary criticism. Each new intepretation is in large measure forged from a contemplation of prior interpretations — their strengths and weaknesses. It represents a rethinking of previous interpretations in terms of a new theory of the author's poetics. My own approach, while selectively exploring and elaborating certain aspects of each of the critical perspectives adumbrated above (particularly the second and fourth), seeks to interpret the *Libro* not as parody of Augustine, but rather as a logical (and constructive instead of deflationary) extension of Augustinian hermeneutics, of his theory of reading.

Each of these modern interpretations — like those of the fifteenth and sixteenth centuries — views the *Libro* essentially either as being didactic (morally or poetically) or as a source of entertainment. As such, each of them is reductionist, for it seeks to explicate the poem according to a univocal perspective.

Rather than pursuing these traditional (exclusivist) forms of *Libro* criticism, my approach focuses on the text's self-proclaimed polysemy (evidenced in the Archpriest's invocations to the reader) viewed as system — which the text itself authorizes us to do. This line of inquiry stems largely from G. B. Gybbon-Monypenny's important study on the intended public of the *mester de clerecía* corpus and its development. In this context he discusses the physical aspect of the Archpriest's book as evidence that it was designed primarily for the individual reader, not for the oral delivery of a *juglar* in the town square to the assembled masses ("The Spanish *Mester de Clerecía*," pp. 236-42).

Of equal importance is Gybbon-Monypenny's observation that oral performance by a minstrel necessarily destroys the distance separating author from narrator-protagonist — a distinction which is of primordial importance to interpretation of the *Libro*: "the whole of the work is cast as an autobiographical narrative, and the protagonist is referred to as 'el arcipreste,' so that we naturally identify him with the author. The author's own comments and digressions are made without any distinction being established in his use of the first person, so that we do not always know whether he speaks as author or protagonist. Clearly a *juglar* could not recite the text of the *Libro* without appearing to claim the author's identity" ("The Spanish *Mester de Clerecía*," p. 239).

Surprisingly, this relationship of author to narrator-protagonist (and the reader's intermediary role in distinguishing between the two) has not been explored in much detail. Nonetheless, the hierarchy of voices must be clearly differentiated since it is essential to our reconstruction of the meaning(s) which the Archpriest builds into his text. As Wayne Booth reminds us in *Critical Understanding*, "some writers choose to dramatize in the text a narrative voice that speaks explicitly for the implied author's norms ... other writers create surrogates who cannot be trusted." [25] Juan Ruiz falls into this latter category, hence the need to distinguish author from narrator-protagonist.

Yet how can we be sure that there exists both a diegetic narrator and an extradiegetic narrator — one who narrates the autobiography and one who resides on another level, projecting values which are different from those of the narrator-protagonist? We know that such a distance exists, as Iser explains, by examining the particular (selective) re-presentation of reality which a given author fabricates in his text: "every literary text in one way or another represents a perspective view of the world put together (though not necessarily typical of) the author. As such, the work is in no way a mere copy of a given world — it constructs a world of its own out of the material available to it. It is the way in which this world is constructed that brings about the perspective intended by the author" (*The Act of Reading*, p. 35).

When, for example, Leo Spitzer remarks of the Archpriest that: "in using this self-incriminating procedure, [he] wished to depict the potential sinner which existed in himself, as in all human beings," [26] he extrapolates from the autobiography to an abstract moral dimension, differentiating the author from the narrator-protagonist, offering us an *exemplum ex negativo*.

---

[25] Wayne C. Booth, *Critical Understanding. The Powers and Limits of Pluralism* (Chicago: University of Chicago Press, 1979), p. 270.
[26] Leo Spitzer, "Note on the Poetic and Empirical 'I' in Medieval Authors," *Traditio*, 4 (1946), 419.

On the other hand, Spitzer minimizes the potential importance of this same author/narrator-protagonist configuration with regard to the role accorded to the individual reader. He writes at length of the text/gloss dichotomy, seeing it basically as an artistic topos whereby (as in the case of Marie de France) the work "sólo alcanzará su perfección con las futuras generaciones de lectores, igual que la Sagrada Escritura, el libro por excelencia, va desplegando ante las sucesivas generaciones su oculta y latente belleza..." ("En torno al arte," pp. 118-19). Marie de France does, indeed, envision glossators of future generations as progressively enriching and revealing the meaning of her *Lais*.[27] However the text/gloss relationship in the *Libro* envisioned by Juan Ruiz is not this sort of diachronic accretion over the centuries, which constitutes the history of the *Libro*'s interpretation. Instead Juan Ruiz — as the text itself attests — is addressing himself to the individual reader's gloss (irrespective of any kind of knowledge or participation in the history of *Libro* interpretation). The final verses of the poem proper (1631-33) — addressed not to scholarly glossators of the future, but to his immediate audience of "ladies and gentlemen" — communicate this idea:

> Fiz'vos pequeño libro de testo, mas la glosa
> non creo que es chica, ante es bien grand prosa;
> ca sobre cada fabla se entiende otra cosa,
> sin lo que se alega en la razón fermosa.

---

[27] As she explains in her prologue:

> Custume fu as ancïens,
> Ceo testimoine Precïens,
> Es livres ke jadis feseient,
> Assez oscurement diseient
> Pur ceus ki a venir esteient
> E ki aprendre les deveient,
> K'i peüssent gloser la lettre
> E de lur sen le surplus mettre. (vv. 9-16)

Ed. Jean Rychner, *Les 'Lais' de Marie de France* (Paris: Champion, 1971), p. 1. See in this regard Alfred Foulet and Karl D. Uitti, "The Prologue to the *Lais* of Marie de France," *Romance Philology*, 35 (1981), 242-49.

> [The custom among the ancients— / as Priscian testifies— / was to speak quite obscurely / in the books they wrote, / so that those who were to come after / and study them / might gloss the letter / and supply its significance from their own wisdom. (*The 'Lais' of Marie de France*, trans., Robert Hanning and Joan Ferrante [Durham, North Carolina: Labyrinth Press, 1978], p. 28.)

De la santidad mucha es muy grand licionario,
mas de juego e de burla es chico breviario;
por ende fago punto e cierro mi almario:
séavos chica burla, solaz e letuario.

Señores, hevos servido con poca sabidoría;
por vos dar solaz a todos, fablévos en juglaría...

(1631a-1633b)

[I have made you a book that is small in terms of text, but the exegesis, I believe, is not brief, rather it is a good big piece of writing; for in respect to each tale, something else is to be understood, apart from the pretty wording.

It is a very big doctrinal book about a great deal of holiness, but it is a small breviary of fun and jokes; so I am making an end and closing my cupboard: may it be for you a brief jest, a delight, and a sweet confection.

Ladies and gentlemen, I have done you service with my scanty learning; to give pleasure to you all, I have addressed you in jocular minstrel fashion.]

Unlike Marie de France, the Archpriest does not envision a diachronic progression towards an increasingly more correct interpretation. He is acutely aware that his work will be understood by some as a didactic treatise,[28] by others as a form of *ars amatoria*,[29] and by still others as *ars poetica*.[30] He is interested in the

---

[28] "compuse este nuevo libro en que son escritas algunas maneras e maestrías e sotilezas engañosas del loco amor del mundo, que usan algunos para pecar. Las quales, leyéndolas e oyéndolas omne o mujer de buen entendimiento, que se quiera salvar, descogerá e obrarlo ha" (9,11). ["I composed this new book in which are written down certain of the ways and tricks and deceitful wiles of the mad and heedless love of this world, which some people employ to commit sin. And if these be read or heard by any man or woman of good understanding, who wishes to be saved, he will make a choice and carry it into effect."]

[29] "porque es umanal cosa el pecar, si algunos — lo que no les consejo — quisieren usar del loco amor, aquí fallarán algunas maneras para ello" (11). ["since to sin is a human thing, if any should choose — which I do not advise them to do — to indulge in mad and heedless love, they will find here some ways for this."]

[30] "compóselo otrossí a dar a algunos leción e muestra de metrificar e rimar e de trobar ca trobas e notas e rimas e ditados e versos fiz' com-

particular interpretation of a given reader *per ipse* — his particular reception within the realm of possible interpretations of the polysemous text which he constructs. Concerned with the reading process on the individual level, Juan Ruiz reflects an awareness of the fact that any text — as Tzvetan Todorov has lucidly articulated — "evokes facts according to two different modes — signification and symbolization ... Signified facts are *understood*: all we need is knowledge of the language in which the text is written. Symbolized facts are *interpreted;* and interpretations vary from one subject to another." [31]

It is the interrelationship of these two modes to the reading subject which Juan Ruiz explores in detail and it is this problematic aspect of textuality which forms the basis of his theory of reading. Reconstruction and definition of this theory of reading (evidenced throughout the text both explicitly and implicitly) is the object of the present study.

---

plidamente, segund que esta ciencia requiere" (13). ["I likewise composed the book in order to give to some people a lesson and example of scanning and rhyming and composing lyrics, for the lyrics and notes and rhymes and poems and verses I composed correctly, as the poetic art requires."]

[31] Tzvetan Todorov, "Reading as Construction," *The Reader in the Text*, eds., Susan R. Sulieman and Inge Crossman (Princeton: Princeton University Press, 1980), p. 73.

As this brief survey of the history of *Libro* criticism attests, interpreters of the twentieth century conform to the three basic critical attitudes in evidence during the fifteenth and sixteenth centuries. For this reason, one might justifiably question the validity of Hans Ulrich Gumbrecht's receptionist approach to it: "una ciencia literaria que merezca su nombre — i.e., que comporte conclusiones intersubjectivas — debe enfocar las diversas reacciones históricas, de las que el mismo texto representa únicamente un punto de partida." ("Aspectos de una historia recepcional del *Libro de buen amor*," *Cuadernos Hispanoamericanos*, 282 [1973], 610.)

II. THE PROSE PROLOGUE AND THE AUGUSTINIAN PARADOX

The lack of critical consensus evidenced by the history of *Libro* scholarship would no doubt have gratified Juan Ruiz, for it attests to the success of his stated objective in writing his book — namely to produce a (necessarily) polysemous text:

> ... este mi libro, a todo omne o mujer, al cuerdo e al non cuerdo, al que entendiere el bien e escogiere salvación e obrare bien amando a Dios, otrossí al que quisiere el amor loco, en la carrera que andudiere, puede a cada uno bien dezir: *Intellectum tibi dabo, et caetera.* (11)

> [... this book of mine, to every man or woman, to the wise and the unwise, to whomsoever may understand the good and choose salvation and do good works loving God, and likewise to whomsoever may desire mad and heedless love on the road which he walks along, to each one it can truly say: *I will give thee understanding, et caetera.*]

The principal object of this study, as outlined in the Introduction, is to demonstrate that the *Libro* is profoundly concerned with the problem of interpretation, that it in fact thematizes the problem of interpretation — functioning as a logical extension of Augustinian hermeneutics. Indeed, it may be shown that Augustine's *Confessions* serves as an important heuristic tool in the elucidation of the Archpriest's problematic text. The presence and import of the various exploitations of the Augustinian subtext — both thematic and structural — will be treated individually in the course of this essay, rather than being summarily enumerated at the present time.

A detailed consideration of the prologue is called for at this point, for it is of prime importance to interpretation of the *Libro,* serving to orient our reading of the text from beginning to end.

Substantial controversy surrounds the prologue: the question of whether or not it existed in the original version of 1330, as well as the question of its potential import for the poem as a whole. Having considered the available manuscript evidence, G. B. Gybbon-Monypenny concludes the following: "Of three possibilities — that the copyist of *G* made a fresh beginning at stanza 11, that the end of the prologue coincided exactly with the end of a folio, or that the first version only began at stanza 11 — the last seems to me the most likely, as it seemed to Menéndez Pidal and Lecoy." [1] Is it not equally plausible to assume that the end of the prologue coincided with the end of a folio, rather than assuming that the 1330 version would begin with stanza 11?

Be that as it may, the purpose of the present discussion is not an attempt to prove or disprove the existence of a prologue in the 1330 version. It is intended instead to illustrate that the prologue which introduces the 1343 version establishes the attitudes which Juan Ruiz sustains throughout both redactions of his text towards his readers and towards the act of reading itself in general.

Three recent analyses of the *Libro*'s prefatory prose shed considerable light on its semantic content as well as on its relationship to the poem as a whole. The studies in question are, in chronological order: Pierre Ullman's "Juan Ruiz's Prologue" [2] (1967); Richard Kinkade's " '*Intellectum tibi dabo*' ... The Function of Free Will in the *Libro de buen amor*" [3] (1970); and Colbert Nepaulsingh's "The Rhetorical Structure of the Prologues to the *Libro de buen amor* and the *Celestina*" [4] (1974). While these pre-

---

[1] G. B. Gybbon-Monypenny, "The Two Versions of the *Libro de buen amor*: The Extent and Nature of the Author's Revision," *Bulletin of Hispanic Studies,* 39 (1962), 209.

[2] Pierre L. Ullman, "Juan Ruiz's Prologue," *MLN,* 82 (1967), 149-70.

[3] Richard P. Kinkade, " '*Intellectum tibi dabo*...': The Function of Free Will in the *Libro de buen amor*," *Bulletin of Hispanic Studies,* 47 (1970), 296-315.

[4] Colbert Nepaulsingh, "The Rhetorical Structure of the Prologues to the *Libro de buen amor* and the *Celestina*," *Bulletin of Hispanic Studies,*

sentations often contradict one another in significant ways, each one contributes to our understanding of the prologue's seminal importance.

Taking as his point of departure Lecoy's classification of the prologue as a "sermon joyeux" ("parodique"), Ullman responds to this interpretation by arguing that it is anachronistic: "the genre [of sermonic parody] was not found in France until the fourteenth century and was not at its height until the fifteenth and sixteenth" ("Juan Ruiz's Prologue," p. 151). Moreover, Ullman asserts, the *sermons joyeux* "have no true rhetorical structure" ("Juan Ruiz's Prologue," p. 151), whereas Juan Ruiz's prolegomenon does — as all three critics agree.

The rhetorical structure discerned by Ullman centers about the debate of free will and determinism. The philosophical tradition of voluntarism begins, as Ullman reminds us, with St. Augustine. *De Trinitate* (Books X and XV, chs. xx and xxi) details his tripartite conception of the soul into *memoria, intelligentia* and *voluntas*. For Augustine, as Ullman properly emphasizes (in contradistinction to Zahareas), [5] there exists a definite correlation between voluntarism and determinism (free will and Divine grace).

Augustine repeatedly tells us — and indeed dramatizes — in the *Confessions* his belief that man's good or bad will determines whether or not he will be susceptible to God's grace. In speaking of the *Libro* and its Augustinian model, Ullman affirms that "the path to salvation is construed voluntaristically" ("Juan Ruiz's Prologue," p. 151). And although his suggestive study does not deal with the *Confessions* but with other Augustinian texts instead, the *Confessions* may be said to function as an emblem of Augustine's belief that "salvation is [to be] construed voluntaristically." It is only once the protagonist actively wills it that the illumination of God's grace becomes possible — not before. [6]

---

51 (1974), 325-34. See also Nicolás Emilio Álvarez, "Análisis estructuralista del Prefacio del *Libro de buen amor*," *Kentucky Romance Quarterly*, 28 (1981), 237-53.

[5] "Augustine denies the efficacy of the human will and asserts the importance of predestination," in Zahareas' view. See his study entitled, "The Stars: Worldly Love and Free Will in the *Libro de buen amor*," *Bulletin of Hispanic Studies*, 42 (1965), 90.

[6] Recalling, for example, his reaction upon reading the Holy Scriptures for the first time, Augustine explains: "non enim sicut modo loquor,

The logical corollary to this epistemological tenet is that evil (bad) will (as well as good will) exists in this world. "Evil is in the eye of the beholder," to use Ullman's words ("Juan Ruiz's Prologue," p. 161). What is revealed to a given individual (his particular interpretation) is determined by his moral state or perspective, his good or bad will. Hence the *Libro*, as Ullman correctly reasons, cannot prevent one from attaining salvation — no matter how much *loco amor* is to be found within the book. Those of good understanding will understand it rightly. Ullman convincingly traces this argument throughout the prologue. However, despite the initial presence of the Augustinian resonance which he perceives, he casts doubt on its function as an informing principle for the Archpriest's text as a whole: "the prologue is not an integral part of the book. It is not initiatory; on the contrary, it was probably added in the second redaction as justification [for the bawdy material contained therein]."[7]

Contrary to Ullman's conclusion regarding possible implications of Augustine's notion of voluntarism for the poem as a whole, it can be demonstrated that this theory of voluntarism — rather than serving merely as camouflage — functions in fact as an opening signal, an informing element which determines the narrative strategies of the entire work to follow. It is Augustine's idea of voluntarism and its bearing on exegesis which Juan Ruiz exploits in his re-writing of the *Confessions* — thereby revealing his own theory of reading.

Richard Kinkade furthers our understanding of the Archpriest's prolegomenon in two important ways. Firstly (largely in response to Zahareas' anachronistic notion) he firmly asserts "Juan Ruiz's orthodox belief in free will" ("*Intellectum tibi dabo*," p. 314),

---

ita sensi, cum attendi ad illam scripturam, sed visa est mihi indigna, quam Tulliane dignitati comparerem." (Augustine's *Confessions*, ed. G. P. Goold [Cambridge: Harvard University Press, 1967], I, 112.) ["These were not the feelings I had when I first read the scriptures. To me they seemed quite unworthy of comparison with the stately prose of Cicero, because I had too much conceit to accept their simplicity and not enough insight to penetrate their depths."] (Augustine's *Confessions*, trans. R. S. Pine-Coffin [Hammondsworth: Penguin, 1961], Bk. III, 5, p. 60.)

[7] "Juan Ruiz's Prologue," p. 154. See also Janet A. Chapman, "Juan Ruiz's Learned Sermon," "*Libro de buen amor*" *Studies*, ed. G. B. Gybbon-Monypenny (London: Tamesis, 1970), pp. 29-52.

which is a mitigating influence over the power of the stars. Moreover, Kinkade maintains that Juan Ruiz adheres to his very orthodox concept of voluntarism throughout the *Libro*. This is indeed the case.

Curiously, one puzzling detail appears in Kinkade's discussion of the prologue, a misattribution of the words *"intellectum tibi dabo,"* which he ascribes to Ecclesiastes (*"Intellectum tibi dabo,"* p. 300). For as the Archpriest explicitly tells us:

> *Intellectum tibi dabo et instruam te in via hac qua gradieris; firmabo super te oculos meos*. El profeta David, por Spíritu Santo fablando, a cada uno de nos dize en el psalmo tricésimo primo del verso dezeno, que es el que primero suso escreví. (5)

> [*I will give thee understanding, and I will instruct thee in this way in which thou shalt go; I will fix my eyes upon thee*. So says the Prophet David, speaking with the Holy Spirit, to each of us in the Thirty-first Psalm (as numbered in the Vulgate Bible), tenth verse, which is the one I wrote above at the beginning.]

It is significant (and strengthens Kinkade's own argument concerning voluntarism) that Juan Ruiz goes to such lengths to attribute the words *"intellectum tibi dabo"* to the Thirty-first Psalm. For this psalm is specifically about voluntarism and its necessary relationship to confession and Grace:

> Delictum meum cognitum tibi feci,
> Et iniustitiam meam non abscondi.
> Dixi: Confitebor adversum me iniustitiam meam Domino;
> Et tu remisisti impietatem peccati mei. [8]

> [I acknowledged my sin to thee, and I did not hide my iniquity; / I said 'I will confess my transgressions to the Lord'; / then thou didst forgive the guilt of my sin. [9]]

The relationship of free will and confession to human nature is the very key to interpretation in the *Libro*.

---

[8] *Biblia Sacra* (Salamanca: Biblioteca de Autores Cristianos, 1965), p. 474.

[9] *The Oxford Annotated Bible* (Oxford: Oxford University Press, 1962), p. 678.

One final study which should be taken into account is Nepaulsingh's analysis, since it elucidates another important dimension of the *Libro*'s complexities. What is at issue here is the rhetorical expertise evidenced by the Archpriest throughout the prologue. Nepaulsingh admirably discusses the various conventions of rhetoric which the Archpriest exploits. He errs, however, in endowing the prologue with exclusively formal importance, for all intents and purposes rejecting its crucially significant semantic dimension: "One debate of questionable relevance, for example, is whether or not Juan Ruiz's prologue should be regarded as a philosophical document that deals with the problem of voluntarism and intellectualism" ("The Rhetorical Structure," p. 325).

Referring to Ullman's study, Nepaulsingh criticizes it for attempting to explicate the prologue in philosophical terms (the dispute between voluntarists and determinists), rather than in rhetorical terms: "... ignoring the Archpriest's rhetorical artistry... Ullman concludes that the prologue is a justification using Augustinian voluntarism to argue that evil is in the eye of the beholder and not in the book" ("The Rhetorical Structure," p. 325).

The findings of one study do not invalidate the other. To the contrary they, as well as Kinkade's, enhance our appreciation of the extreme care with which the Archpriest conceived his book.

In the *Libro* — beginning with the prose introduction — Juan Ruiz establishes and recasts the *Confessions* both formally and thematically. This re-writing of Augustine is initiated as the Archpriest adopts for his point of departure a paradox which is inherent in the Augustinian text: i.e., the discrepancy between, on the one hand, Augustine's reiterated belief that what one comprehends in a work (he is thinking specifically of Scripture) depends on his moral state [10] (hence that a given text will be subject to many dif-

---

[10] This is a recurring theme in the *Confessions*. For example in Book III, 12, Augustine's mother approaches a bishop, asking him to instruct her wayward son in the true religion. He does not grant her wish, as Augustine explains:

> "quem cum illa femina rogasset, ut dignaretur mecum conloqui, et refellere errores meos, et dedocere me mala ac docere bona — faciebat enim hoc, quos forte idoneos invenisset — noluit ille, prudenter sane, quantum sensi postea. respondit enim me adhuc esse indocilem, et quod inflatus essem novitate haeresis illius, et

ferent interpretations); on the other hand, that it is possible to write his *Confessions* in order not only to achieve his personal salvation, but that of his "universal reader" as well. The *Confessions* is presented simultaneously as a record of Augustine's own conversion and as a paradigm for his universal (Everyman) reader, as a "conversion mechanism," so to speak. However, since by Augustine's own admission, no universal reader (with a univocal interpretation) exists — his text cannot logically function as a conversion mechanism for those readers who are not already so inclined or predisposed.

While this logical discrepancy is not problematic for Augustine, for Juan Ruiz it is. Indeed, it is precisely this paradox (positing the existence of a universal reader, but realizing that he doesn't exist) which generates the bifocal tension found within the *Libro*.

The faculty of memory is of essential importance to the reading-theory projected by Augustine and Juan Ruiz alike. Memory is the key which determines both the form and content of the *Confessions*. Memory serves as a form of mimesis for Augustine, both as representation of "things which actually happened" and of "things as they are in general." The *Confessions* is literally a narrative of memories in which Augustine tells us in Book III, "ego sum, qui memini, ego animus" (118) ["I am investigating myself, my memory, my mind" (223).] [11] From the perspective of the time

---

    nonnullis quaestiunculis iam multos inperitos exagitassem, sicut illa indicaverat ei" (140, 142).
    [My mother asked him, as a favour, to have a talk with me, so that he might refute my errors, drive the evil out of my mind, and replace it with good. He often did this when he found suitable pupils, but he refused to do it for me — a wise decision, as I afterwards realized. He told her that I was still unripe for instruction because, as she had told him, I was brimming over with the novelty of the heresy and had already upset a great many people with my casuistry. (69)]

[11] In this connection see E. Michael Gerli's very suggestive analysis of Augustine's *De Magistro* and possible implications for the Archpriest's pedagogy in "*Recta voluntas est bonus amor*: St. Augustine and the Didactic Structure of the *Libro de buen amor*," *Romance Philology*, 35 (1982), 500-508; and Dayle Seidenspinner-Núñez's discussion of Augustine's *De Doctrina Christiana* in *The Allegory of Good Love: Parodic Perspectivism in the 'Libro de buen amor'* (Berkeley: University of California Press, 1981), pp. 10 ff. Both of these works appeared after my study was already in press. Thus it was not possible to take their numerous interesting observations into account here in a detailed manner.

of writing he is analyzing his past life (the time of the narrative), the "now" of the believing Christian versus the "then" of the reprobate. For example, he examines his motivation in stealing the pears from the pear tree, which (as he now realizes) he stole, not because he was hungry, but simply because he delighted in committing sin:

> ... nam decerpta proieci epulatus inde solam iniquitatem, qua laetabar fruens. nam et si quid illorum pomorum intravit in os meum, condimentum ibi facinus erat. (II, 82, 84)

> [For no sooner had I picked them than I threw them away, and tasted nothing in them but my own sin, which I relished and enjoyed. If any part of those pears passed my lips, it was the sin that gave it flavour. (49)]

Like Augustine, Juan Ruiz also ponders the power of human memory at the beginning of his book, but he — significantly — arrives at the opposite conclusion:

> ... dize el salmista: *Cogitationes hominum vanae sunt* ... E aún digo que viene de la pobredad de la memoria, que no está instructa del buen entendimiento, assí que non puede amar el bien nin acordarse d'ello para lo obrar. E viene otrossí esto por razón que la natura humana ... más aparejada e inclinada es al mal que al bien, e a pecado que a bien .. tener todas las cosas en la memoria e non olvidar algo, más es de la Divinidad que de la humanidad. (9)

> [... the psalmist says: *The thoughts of men are vain* ... And I further say that this comes from (deficiency) of (...) memory, which is not instructed by (...) good understanding, so that it cannot love the good, nor remember it in order to do it. And also this comes about because human nature ... is more prepared for, and inclined towards, the bad than the good, and more to sin than to goodness ... to keep all things in the memory and not to forget, is more divine than human.]

For Juan Ruiz, thus, memory lacks the corrective power with which Augustine invests it. And as a result, the Archpriest decides to write his book entirely from the perspective of a sinner, whose poor memory makes him continually susceptible to earthly temptation: "yo... só omne, como otro pecador" ["I am a man, like any other sinner"] he explains in stanza 76. At the time of writing he is as unresistant to sin as he was during the time of the narrative.

Indeed, the prologue to the *Libro* constitutes an inversion in miniature of the narrative strategies employed by Augustine in the elucidation of his theory of the acquisition of knowledge through memory in the *Confessions*. Namely Augustine recounts his wayward past and subsequent conversion as a necessary means of attaining the moral excellence that is the essential starting-point for proper scriptural exegesis — which the last three books of the *Confessions* treat in detail.

Significantly, Juan Ruiz reverses this procedure — beginning his prologue with the words "*Intellectum tibi dabo*," taken from the Thirty-first Psalm, which deals with confession. What follows in the remainder of the prose prologue is a lengthy exegesis of the quotation from Psalms, which illustrates not only the narrator's exegetical mastery — but at the same time — his profound skepticism regarding the didactic efficacy of exemplary literature per se:

> Dios sabe que la mi intención non fue de lo fazer por dar manera de pecar nin por mal dezir; mas fue por reduzir a toda persona a memoria buena de bien obrar e dar ensiemplo de buenas costumbres, e castigos de salvación... Empero, porque es umanal cosa el pecar, si algunos — lo que non les consejo — quisieren usar del loco amor, aquí fallaran algunas maneras para ello. (11)

> [God knows that my intention was not to compose the book in order to provide ways to commit sin or speak evil, but was to guide everyone back to good memory of good deeds, and to give examples of good conduct and admonitions for salvation... However, since to sin is a human thing, if any should choose — which I do not advise them to do — to indulge in mad and heedless love, they will find here some ways for this.]

This fundamental epistemological discrepancy between the two authors is aptly illustrated by the Archpriest's re-writing of Augustine's famous pear tree incident (sts. 153d-154d):

> ... a muchas [dueñas] serví mucho, que nada acabecí.
>
> Comoquier que he provado mi signo ser atal:
> en servir a las dueñas punar e non en ál;
> pero *aunque non goste la pera del peral,
> en estar a la sombra es plazer comunal.* [12]
>
> [(I have served many ladies), yet nothing have I accomplished.
>
> Although I have proven that my natal destiny was this: to put my efforts into serving (...) ladies and into nothing else (i.e., and never to succeed in possessing them); nevertheless, *although one may not taste the pear of the pear tree, just being in its shade is a pleasure for everyone.*]

Two important transformations of the global Augustinian model are at issue here. First, unlike Augustine, the Archpriest does not engage in persuasive Christian rhetoric (the narrative blueprint for the *Confessions*), he is not explicitly trying to convert his readers because for him reading cannot logically perform this function. Finding the Augustinian theory of reading to be a logical paradox, Juan Ruiz, rather than offering a model of salvation, offers instead a parable of the human condition — a representative text in place of the imitative one. In other words, he depicts man as he really is instead of man as he should strive to become.

This first transformation is concretized by the symbolic function of the trees. For while Augustine unequivocally rejects the pear tree for the shade of the fig tree at the moment of his conversion, Juan Ruiz — as he confesses to us — remains perpetually in the shade of the pear tree (the lyric tree *par excellence*). Explaining the generative significance for the reader of Augustine's choice of the fig tree, John Freccero writes as follows:

> The fig tree in the garden of Milan, in the eighth book of the *Confessions,* for all of its historicity, is at the same time meant to represent the broader pattern of salvation history for all Christians. The moment represents the revela-

---
[12] Emphasis mine.

tion of God's word at a particular time and place, recapitulating the Christ event in a particular soul. Behind that fig tree stands a whole series of anterior images pointing back to Genesis. [13]

Conversely, as Marcia Colish explains, the pear tree for Augustine signifies the "love of sin," functioning as a paradigm of sinfulness, as "an inverted reflection of the perfect love of God." [14]

Hence in the Augustinian system, the pear tree represents the Tree of the Knowledge of Good and Evil. And by opting for this tree, the Archpriest presents himself (and every man) as a postlapsarian Adam. Moreover, this is probably why he uses the name "Juan Ruiz" which is akin to the English "John Doe." [15]

The second fundamental Augustinian transformation in question has to do with the Archpriest's self-presentation as a failed lover (quite unlike Augustine). While Augustine presents himself until the time of his conversion as a potentially successful and passionate lover, Juan Ruiz presents himself as a persistently blundering, comical would-be lover (implicitly yet unmistakably exemplifying human folly). It is of paramount importance to note that each episode involving the protagonist's pursuit of women — while an amorous failure — explicitly leads to the writing of poetry. [16] While an amorous failure, he is a poetic success. Although a failed lover, he is at the same time, as he repeatedly reminds us, an ingenious poet, displaying not only an impressive degree of

---

[13] John Freccero, "The Fig Tree and the Laurel: Petrarch's Poetics," *Diacritics*, 5 (1975), 36.

[14] Marcia L. Colish, *The Mirror of Language: A Study in the Medieval Theory of Knowledge* (New Haven: Yale University Press, 1968), p. 28.

[15] In this connection, see Moffatt, "The Evidence of Early Mentions of the Archpriest," p. 41.

[16] So that we do not miss the point of this simultaneous amorous failure and poetic success, the Archpriest describes himself in stanza 575 (immediately after the god of Love has left) as follows:

Yo, Juan Ruiz, el sobredicho arcipreste de Hita,
pero que mi coraçón de trobar non se quita,
nunca fallé dueña como a vos Amor pinta,
nin creo que la falle en toda esta cohita.

[I, Juan Ruiz, the aforementioned Archpriest of Hita, even though my heart never ceases from making songs, have never found such a woman as Love has painted for you, nor do I think I shall in all this block of houses.]

technical mastery but a profound knowledge of literary traditions and conventions, for he simultaneously manipulates these poetic concepts and skills with a great degree of creativity. He is thus a successful love poet indeed. Similarly, while a failed Christian, he is a successful Christian poet, capable of writing devotional poetry which is as distinguished as his amorous poetry.

As a result, the Archpriest valorizes "poetic truth" as a means of reflecting (and perhaps even of attaining) "religious truth." Whether or not the reader interprets the *Libro*'s poetry as containing religious truth is dependent upon his moral perspective (an adaptation and enlarging of the Augustinian hermeneutic system). This broad — constructive — function of poetry in the *Libro* is generated by the Archpriest in sharp contrast to Augustine, for whom poetic fiction is, quite simply, a "moral vacuum," as he explains on numerous occasions in the *Confessions*.[17] Juan Ruiz may thus be said to "correct" poetically the (for him) limited Augustinian attitude towards secular poetry.

The pride exhibited by Juan Ruiz with respect to his poetic virtuosity is revealed from the very beginning of his text — in the prose prologue. For there he explicitly presents his poem as offering two kinds of models. He writes: (1) not only "por reduzir a toda persona a memoria buena de bien obrar e dar ensiemplo de buenas costumbres, e castigos de salvación" ["to guide everyone back to good memory of good deeds, and to give examples of good conduct and admonitions for salvation"], as he affirms (p. 11), but in addition (2) "compóselo otrossí a dar a algunos lecion e muestra de metrificar e rimar e de trobar, ca trobas e notas e rimas e ditados e versos fiz' complidamente, segund que esta ciencia requiere" (13) ["I likewise composed the book in order to give to some people a lesson and example of scanning and rhyming and composing lyrics, for the lyrics and notes and rhymes and poems and verses I composed correctly, as the poetic art requires."]

---

[17] E.g., Bk. I, xiii, where Augustine speaks at length of the dangers of fiction: "at enim vela pendent liminibus grammaticarum scholarum, sed non illa magis honorem secreti quam tegimentum erroris significant" (40). ["It is true that curtains are hung over the entrances to the schools where literature is taught, but they are not so much symbols in honor of mystery as veils concealing error" (34).]

These are the two dimensions of the Augustinian text which Juan Ruiz coherently recasts in the *Libro* in order to underscore his own theory of reading — more precisely, his own attitude towards the parameters of exemplary discourse — and of fictional discourse as well.

III. TWO FIGURAL READINGS

Numerous points of contact (both formal and thematic) are shared by the *Confessions* and the *Libro* in addition to those discussed above. Both texts are, first of all, inscribed prayers within which are related the protagonists' exploits. Whether or not one believes that the prose prologue existed in the 1330 version, both stanzas 1 and 11 (like the last sentence of the prose) are invocations to the Lord:

> Señor Dios, que a los judiós, pueblo de perdición,
> saqueste de cabtivo, de poder de Faraón;
> a Daniel saqueste del pozo de Babilón:
> saca a mí, coitado, d'esta mala presión. (st. 1)

> [Lord God, who delivered the Jews, accursed race, from captivity, from under the power of Pharaoh; who delivered Daniel from the pit of Babylon: deliver me, racked by anguish, from this dire prison.]

> Dios Padre, e Dios Fijo e Dios Espíritu Santo:
> El que nació de Virgen esfuércenos de tanto
> que siempre lo loemos en prosa e en canto;
> sea de nuestras almas cobertura e manto. (st. 11)

> [God the Father, and God the Son, and God the Holy Ghost: may He who was born of the Virgin so strengthen us that we may ever praise Him in verse and song, may he be the covering and mantle of our souls.]

Likewise, the prologue ends with the words: "comencé mi libro en el nombre de Dios, e tomé el verso primero del salmo, que es de la Santa Trinidad e de la fe católica, que es *Quicumque vult,* el vesso que dize: *Ita Deus Pater, Deus Filius, et caetera*" (13)

["I therefore began my book in the name of God, and took the first verse of the canticle which is of the Holy Trinity and of the Catholic faith, which is *Whosoever wishes,* the verse that reads: *Verily God the Father, God the Son, et cetera.*"] The two surviving manuscripts of the *Libro* which contain st. 1633 (MSS *S* and *T*), both end the narrative proper with the same request of the reader:

> Señores, hevos servido con poca sabidoría;
> por vos dar solaz a todos, fablévos en juglaría;
> yo un galardón vos pido: que por Dios, en romería,
> digades un paternoster por mi e avemaría.

> [Ladies and gentlemen, I have done you service with my scanty learning; to give pleasure to you all, I have addressed you in jocular minstrel fashion; I beg a reward of you: that in the name of God, on a pilgrimage, you say a Lord's Prayer for me and a Hail Mary.]

The inscription of a poetic text within the form of a prayer is certainly not unique to Juan Ruiz, this practice of course being a constant within the *mester de clerecía* corpus which began in the thirteenth century.[1] Nonetheless, the degree of similarity (and of difference) between the *Libro*'s invocation and that of the *Confessions* is important, meriting close consideration.

Not only is the *Confessions* inscribed within a prayer, but its opening reveals a great deal about the way in which Augustine intends for his text to be read:

---

[1] E.g., the *Libro de Apolonio*:

> En el nombre de Dios y de Santa María,
> si ellos me guiassen estudiar querría,
> componer un romance de nueva maestría
> del buen rey Apolonio y de su cortesía. (st. 1)

Ed. Manuel Alvar, *Libro de Apolonio* (Valencia: Castalia, 1977), vol. II, 19.

> [In God's and Holy Mary's name, / If they will guide me, / it is my aim / In a new style of poetry / To tell of a king's courtesy.] (*The Book of Apollonius,* trans., Raymond L. Grismer and Elizabeth Atkins [Minneapolis: University of Minnesota Press, 1936], p. 3.)

The *Libro de Alexandre* and virtually all of Berceo's poems begin in a similar fashion.

> Magnus es, domine, et laudabilis valde ... da mihi, domine, scire et intellegere, utrum sit prius invocare te an laudare te, et scire te prius sit an invocare te. sed quis te invocat nesciens te? aliud enim pro alio potest invocare nesciens (2).
>
> [Can any praise be worthy of the Lord's majesty? ... Grant me, Lord, to know and understand whether a man is first to pray to you for help or to praise you, and whether he must know you before he can call you to his aid. If he does not know you, how can he pray to you? For he may call for some other help, mistaking it for yours (21).]

As is evident from these opening remarks, Augustine is interested not only in praising the Lord but, to an equal degree, in discovering His true nature — to the extent that this is humanly possible: "If he [man] does not know you, how can he pray to you?" Indeed, the *Confessions* is a profoundly self-analytical text which seeks to uncover and describe God's true nature so that we can better understand it in order to praise Him more suitably. Such intense inquiry into the nature of God is not of central importance to Juan Ruiz's text, which concerns itself primarily with a depiction of man's true (basically un-self-reflective) nature. This major difference will be elaborated at length in the pages to follow because of its bearing upon the reading-theory of each author.

Continuing with the similarities evidenced at the beginning of the two texts under consideration, we find that each one involves a program of quotations from Psalms which is glossed by the narrative itself. Both authors plead for divine intercession by means of their writings. Finally, Juan Ruiz and Augustine, in their capacity as autobiographers, draw upon the poetic resources of romance.[2] Namely, in their respective works each author may be said to juxtapose secular romance (love-quest) with "sacred romance" (religious quest).[3]

---

[2] "... in combining two of the standard types of medieval erotic literature — the didactic allegory and the *roman* — Juan Ruiz was inevitably led to choose the first person for his narrative" (G. B. Gybbon-Monypenny, "Autobiography in the *Libro de buen amor* in the Light of Some Literary Comparisons," *Bulletin of Hispanic Studies*, 34 [1957], 67).

[3] Romance is, strictly speaking, self-referential. However, as Northrop Frye points out: "In every period of history certain ascendant values are

In the case of Augustine, the love-quest — his obsessive carnal desire — leads him ultimately to religious-quest (by means of the all-important faculty of memory). He undergoes a linear (explicitly sequential, chronological) progression — beginning in a state of moral impoverishment that leads to a period of extended psychomaquia during which he seeks (and ultimately attains) Christian truth. The progressive (linear) nature of this quest is repeatedly emphasized by the author, who deliberately traces the progression from infancy to adulthood, designating each stage in his spiritual development according to his chronological age at that particular moment: Book I treats of his infancy; Book II of his boyhood; Books III and IV, of his life between the ages of 19 and 27; Books V, VI and VII, until the age of 30; Book VIII, the years 31-33 (culminating in the christological age, which coincides with Augustine's conversion). With the conversion scene and the death of Monica in the protagonist's thirty-third year (Book IX), the narrator ceases to chart out his spiritual growth in terms of chronology. There is no longer any need for such temporal correlation. Augustine qua author has successfully exploited temporal references in order to illustrate the generative potential which the faculty of human memory provides according to his system. It is his contemplation, his dwelling upon past actions and their motivations — such as the pear tree incident — which allows him to refine retrospectively his moral condition to the point where he becomes receptive to God's Word. It is important to note that it is not reading per se which converts him when he hears the words "Tolle, lege" in Book VIII. For he had been a reader of Scripture many times before that moment. [4] It is instead his altered moral perspec-

---

accepted by society and are embodied in its serious literature. Usually this process includes some form of kidnapped romance, that is, romance formulas used to reflect certain ascendant religious or social ideals" (Northrop Frye, *The Secular Scripture* [Cambridge: Harvard University Press, 1978], pp. 29-30).

[4] For example, in Book VI Augustine writes: "Gaudebam etiam, quod vetera scripta legis et prophetarum iam non illo oculo mihi legenda proponerentur, quo antea videbantur absurda, cum arguebam tamquam ita sentintes sanctos tuos; verum autem non ita sentiebant. (278) ... eoque mihi illa venerabilior et sacrosancta fide dignior apparebat auctoritas, quo et omnibus ad legendum esset in promptu, et secreti sui dignitatem in intellectu profundiore servaret, verbis apertissimis et humillimo genere loquendi se

tive — arrived at through the power of memory, of mental reflection — which allows him to understand the power of Christianity for the first time in the garden at Milan:

> ego sub quadam fici arbore stravi me nescio quomodo, et dimisi habenas lacrimis, et prorumperunt flumina oculorum meorum ... et ecce audio vocem de vicina domo cum cantu dicentis, et crebro repetentis, quasi pueri an puellae, nescio: 'tolle lege, tolle lege' ... repressoque impetu lacrimarum surrexi, nihil aliud interpretans divinitus mihi iuberi, nisi ut aperirem codicem et legerem quod primum caput invenissem. audieram enim de Antonio, quod ex evangelica lectione, cui forte supervenerat, admonitus fuerit, tamquam sibi diceretur quod legebatur: vade, vende omnia, quae habes, da pauperibus et habebis thesaurum in caelis; et veni, sequere me: et tali oraculo confestim ad te esse conversum. itaque concitus redii in eum locum, ubi sedebat Alypius: ibi enim posueram codicem apostoli, cum inde surrexeram. arripui, aperui et legi in silentio capitulum, quo primum coniecti sunt oculi mei: non in comissationibus et ebrietatibus, non in cubilibus et impudicitiis, non in contentione et aemulatione, sed induite dominum Iesum Christum, et carnis providentiam ne feceritis in concupiscentiis. nec ultra volui legere, nec opus erat. statim quippe cum fine huiusce sententiae, quasi luce securitatis infusa cordi meo, omnes dubitationis tenebrae diffugerunt. (462, 464)

> [I flung myself down beneath a fig tree and gave way to the tears which now streamed from my eyes ... Whether it was the voice of a boy or girl I cannot say, but again and again it repeated the refrain 'Take it and read, take it and read' ... I stemmed my flood of tears and stood up, telling myself that this could only be a divine command to open my book of Scripture and read the first passage

---

cunctis praebens, et exercens intentionem eorum, qui non sunt leves corde" (284) ["I was glad ... that at last I had been shown how to interpret the ancient Scriptures of the law and the prophets in a different light from that which had previously made them seem absurd, when I used to criticize your saints for holding beliefs which they had never really held at all (115) ... the authority of Scripture should be respected and accepted with the purest faith, because while all can read it with ease, it also has a deeper meaning in which its great secrets are locked away. Its plain language and simple style make it accessible to everyone, and yet it absorbs the attention of the learned" (117).]

on which my eyes should fall. For I had heard the story of Antony, and *I remembered* [5] how he had happened to go into a church while the Gospel was being read and had taken it as a counsel addressed to himself when he heard the words 'Go home and sell all that belongs to you. Give it to the poor, and so the treasure you have shall be in heaven; then come back and follow me' (Matt. 19:21). By this divine pronouncement he had at once been converted to you.

So I hurried back to the place where Alypius was sitting, for when I stood up to move away I had put down the book containing Paul's Epistles. I seized it and opened it, and in silence I read the first passage on which my eyes fell: 'Not in revelling and drunkenness, not in lust and wantonness, not in quarrels and rivalries. Rather, arm yourself with the Lord Jesus Christ; spend no more thought on nature and nature's appetites.' I had no wish to read more and no need to do so. For in an instant, as I came to the end of the sentence, it was as though the light of confidence flooded into my heart and all the darkness of doubt was dispelled (177-78).]

Concerning this extraordinary scene of conversion John Freccero makes two observations which are of central importance to the study of reading-theory in Augustine and Juan Ruiz. The first point articulated by Freccero concerning conversion in the *Confessions* is that "conversion is always a literary event" ("Fig Tree," p. 36). Indeed, the literariness of the conversion (the power of reading) is emphasized in Book VIII not only with reference to Augustine's conversion, but also in the three other conversion scenes recounted therein. The first conversion which we learn of in Book VIII is that of two Roman officials who were converted as a result of reading a passage from the life of St. Antony: "invenisse ibi codicem, in quo scripta erat vita Antonii. quam legere coepit unus eorum, et mirari et accendi, et inter legendum meditari arripere talem vitam et relicta militia saeculari servire tibi" (434) ["They found a book containing the life of St. Antony. One of them began to read it and was so fascinated and thrilled by the story that even before he had finished reading he conceived the idea of taking upon himself the same kind of life and abandoning

---

[5] Emphasis mine.

his career in the world — both he and his friend were officials in the service of the State — in order to become your servant" (167).] Thus the conversion of the first man is directly responsible for the conversion of the second.

The power of this (double) literary conversion effects yet another — that of the fiancées of the former Roman officials: "habebant ambo sponsas: quae posteaquam hoc audierunt, dicaverunt etiam ipsae virginitatem tibi" (436). ["Both of these men were under a promise of marriage, but once the two women heard what had happened, they too dedicated their virginity to you" (168).]

The third conversion effected by the act of reading is Augustine's own (reproduced above). In connection with his conversion — at the very moment of his illumination — it is important to note that he remembers the story of St. Antony's conversion, which was brought about as the Gospel was being read. [6]

Thus reading (in conjunction with memory, hence reflective reading) is, in the Augustinian epistemology, an essential prerequisite for spiritual illumination. Moreover as the aforementioned scenes of conversion reveal, reading in the *Confessions* functions figurally. St. Antony functions figurally as model for the Roman officials, for the two women, and for Augustine himself. Likewise, St. Antony was moved to the point of conversion as a direct result of the reading of the Gospels. One reader functions as model for the next in a sort of paradigmatic chain of readers who achieve a literary understanding of God's relationship to the world.

Clearly, we as readers of the *Confessions* are meant to react to it precisely as the converts in Book VIII reacted to Scripture. Scripture and its exegesis function as model for the *Confessions,* as Augustine demonstrates both in the narrative of Books I-IX and in the interpretation of Scripture which occupies Books X-XIII.

---

[6] "repressoque impetu lacrimarum surrexi, nihil aliud interpretans divinitus mihi iuberi, nisi ut aperirem codicem et legerem quod primum caput invenissem. audieram enim de Antonio, quod ex evangelica lectione, cui forte supervenerat, admonitus fuerit, tamquam sibi diceretur quod legebatur..." [464]) ["I stemmed my flood of tears and stood up, telling myself that this could only be a divine command to open my book of Scripture and read the first passage on which my eyes should fall. For I had heard the story of Antony, and I remembered how he had happened to go into a church while the Gospel was being read and had taken it as a counsel addressed to himself when he heard the words..." (177)]

While these two parts of the Augustinian text are often viewed as being only loosely related to one another, they are, as Eugene Vance explains, profoundly interrelated.[7] One cannot begin to interpret Scripture correctly unless he first understands his role in God's cosmos. This conviction is the justification for the narration of the events of Augustine's life, as he tells us.[8]

The generative function of reading in the *Confessions,* as in Scripture, is dramatically illustrated for us by Augustine at the moment of his conversion. For having just understood the relevance of the Biblical passage to his particular life (and therefore having undergone conversion), he immediately hands the Bible to his friend. "This [moment] points to his newly acquired vocation," as Freccero notes, "for he then passes the Bible to Alypius, thereby suggesting that his own text is to be applied metaleptically to the reader himself as part of the unfolding of God's Word in time" ("Fig Tree," pp. 36-37).

The implied reader and the inscribed reader of the *Confessions* are thus designed to merge into one community of persons, namely those who are susceptible to the power of Christian truth — those who read with charity.[9]

The *Confessions* is intended not simply as a record of Augustine's own life and conversion but, to an equal (or greater) extent, as a potentially active force in the lives of others insofar as it provides a model of reading. Speaking of his inscribed readers from the early pages of his text, Augustine explicitly reveals this didactic purpose: "cui narro haec? neque enim tibi, deus meus, sed apud te narro haec generi meo, generi humano, quantulacumque

---

[7] See Eugene Vance, "Augustine's *Confessions* and the Grammar of Selfhood," *Genre,* 4 (1973), 1-28.

[8] The text contains numerous digressions from the story line such as the following: "Recordari volo transactas foeditates meas, et carnales corruptiones animae meae, non quod eas amem, sed ut amem te, deus meus. amore amoris tui facio istuc, recolens vias meas nequissimas in amaritudine recogitationis meae..." (64) ["I must now carry my thoughts back to the abominable things I did in those days, the sins of the flesh which defiled my soul. I do this, my God, not because I love those sins, but so that I may love you. For love of your life I shall retrace my wicked ways. The memory is bitter, but it will help me to savour your sweetness..." (43)]

[9] See Bk. X, iii, pp. 76-80 for a discussion by Augustine of those readers who will read his *Confessions* with charity.

ex particula incidere potest in istas meas litteras. et ut quid hoc? ut videlicet ego et quisquis haec legit cogitemus, de quam profundo clamandum sit ad te. et quid propius auribus tuis, si cor confitens et vita ex fide est?" (70). ["I need not tell all this (the narration of his past life) to you, my God, but in your presence I tell it to my own kind, to those other men, however few, who may perhaps pick up this book. And I tell it so that I and all who read my words may realize the depths from which we are to cry to you. Your ears will surely listen to the cry of a penitent heart which lives the life of faith" (45).]

Finally, Augustine qua narrator reinforces the figural status of his text by presenting himself qua protagonist as a Biblical avatar. To take one example of this extensive practice, he speaks in Book VI of his mother's despair at his religious waywardness as follows: "tamen ei cum indicassem non me quidem iam esse Manichaeum, sed neque Catholicum Christianum, non, quasi inopinatum aliquid audierit, exiluit laetitia, cum iam secura fieret ex ea parte miseriae meae, in qua me, tamquam mortuum, resuscitandum tibi flebat, et feretro cogitationis offerebat, ut diceres filio viduae; Iuvenis, tibi dico, surge: et revivesceret et inciperet loqui, et traderes illum matri suae" (264, 266). ["I told her that I was not a Catholic Christian, but at least I was no longer a Manichee... in her prayers to you she wept for me as though I were dead, but she also knew that you would recall me to life. In her heart she offered me to you as though I were laid out on a bier, waiting for you to say to the widow's son, 'Young man, I say to you, stand up.' And he would get up and begin to speak, and you would give him back to his mother (cf. Luke 7:14, 15)" (111).]

The Biblical subtext — the figurative Christian hermeneutic — which is built into the *Confessions* is meant to prepare the reader for the last four Books, which deal specifically with proper Scriptural exegesis. More precisely, Book X deals with the power of human memory while Books XI-XIII explore the rich, multi-faceted meaning of Genesis. Taking a given verse from the Book of Genesis, Augustine offers what amounts to a catalogue of the varying interpretations of numerous exegetes. From this inventory of diverging opinions he concludes that they are all admissible, given that each of the readers approaches his text with charity.

Thus "dull minds" (282) as well as keen ones can profit from the exercise of reading. Augustine goes to considerable lengths to express his belief in the existence of a whole corpus of possible correct interpretations, as he explains, for example, in Book XII: "dum ergo quisque conatur id sentire in scripturis sanctis, quod in eis sensit ille qui scripsit, quid mali est, si hoc sentiat, quod tu, lux omnium veridicarum mentium, ostendis verum esse, etiamsi non hoc sensit ille, quem legit, cum et ille verum nec tamen hoc senserit?" [330]). ["Provided ... that each of us tries as best he can to understand in the Holy Scriptures what the writer meant by them, what harm is there if a reader believes what you, the Light of all truthful minds, show him to be the true meaning? It may not even be the meaning which the writer had in mind, and yet he too saw in them a true meaning, different though it may have been from this" (296).]

As proof of his valorization of the polysemy of Scripture, Augustine (in Book XII) explicitly informs his reader that the *Confessions,* like the Bible, is polysemous in nature and that each reader will interpret it according to his particular understanding (as with Scripture): "ego certe, quod intrepidus de meo corde pronuntio, si ad culmen auctoritatis aliquid scriberem, sic mallem scribere, ut, quod veri quisque de his rebus capere posset, mea verba resonarent, quam ut unam veram sententiam ad hoc apertius ponerem, ut excluderem ceteras..." (366, 368) ["For my part I declare resolutely and with all my heart that if I were called upon to write a book which was to be vested with the highest authority, I should prefer to write it in such a way that a reader could find re-echoed in my words whatever truths he was able to apprehend. I would rather write in this way than impose a single true meaning so explicitly that it would exclude all others..." (308)]. He is here speaking of the spectrum of possible Christian interpretations.

Thus the reader of the *Confessions* is actually meant to replace the protagonist as object of (self) study. The text moves from being mimetic in the sense of representing the particular events of Augustine's life — to being imitative, offering a model for salvation. This narrative shift is definitively effected in Book VIII, the midpoint in the narration, the moment of conversion.

As this discussion of Augustinian hermeneutics makes manifest, the *Confessions* is, among other things, a document of persuasive Christian rhetoric which is exemplary — affording a model of reading which is intended to convert others by the very act of reading. In its profoundest sense, the *Confessions* is a work about reading-theory and the problematics of interpretation.

INTERPRETATION IN THE *Libro*

In the *Libro* Juan Ruiz self-consciously addresses himself to several of the basic hermeneutic issues which Augustine raises and responds to in the *Confessions*. His particular working-out of these issues, however, takes on a radically different form.

This difference in reading-theory stems, as discussed above in the analysis of the Archpriest's prologue, [10] from what Juan Ruiz perceives to be a problem, a fallacy or illogicality in the Augustinian system of reading. The discrepancy in Augustine's logic is no mystery. [11] Clearly, what allows him to overcome what (for him) is only an ostensible paradox is his belief in the power of exemplary literature, specifically the power of the Word of Holy Scripture.

For the Archpriest, human memory lacks the instructive dimension with which Augustine endows it, as the above discussion of the *Libro*'s prologue reveals. This belief in the frailty of man's memory is in fact elaborated at considerable length in the prologue. Because human memory is "feeble" (8), the disciplines of painting, writing and sculpture were invented as a corrective device for the deficiencies of our memory. Pondering the psalmist's assertion that *"cogitationes hominum vanae sunt"* (9) ["the thoughts of men are vain"] the Archpriest affirms that such is indeed the case — owing to the poorness of man's memory ("la memoria del omne desleznadera es" [9]), coupled with the fact that in addition man is more inclined towards evil than good ("la natura umana... más aparejada e inclinada es al mal que al bien, e a pecado que a

---

[10] See pp. 23-35 above.
[11] For a discussion of the paradoxical assumptions at the heart of Augustine's autobiographical enterprise, see Eugene Vance's important articles: "Augustine's *Confessions* and the Grammar of Selfhood" (cited above), and his "Le moi comme langage: Saint Augustin et l'autobiographie," *Poétique*, 14 (1973): 163-78.

bien" [9]). Expatiating on this idea, Juan Ruiz further explains that "éstas son algunas de las razones por que son fechos los libros de la ley e del derecho, e de castigos e de costumbres, e de otras ciencias. Otrossí fueron la pintura e la escritura e las imágenes primeramente falladas, por razón que la memoria del omne desleznadera es: esto dize el Decreto. Ca tener todas las cosas en la memoria e non olvidar algo, más es de la Divinidad que de la umanidad..." (9) ["these are some of the reasons why men have written books of commandments and law, and of admonitions and good conduct, and other sorts of wisdom. Likewise painting and writing and sculpture were first discovered because man's memory is feeble: thus says the Decretal. For to keep all things in the memory and not to forget, is more divine than human."] Juan Ruiz is quite deliberate in making his point about the limitations of exemplary presentation insofar as the reader is concerned. Although the exemplary media which he mentions are intended to instruct us, since human memory is entirely flawed — as Juan Ruiz reminds us — we are hardly susceptible to the lessons furnished by their didactic mode. It is thus with a certain degree of irony — and with Augustine in mind — that the Archpriest contradicts what he has just said about the invention of the exemplary media and their inefficacy due to the weak power of human memory, affirming that: "los de poco entendimiento non se perderán, ca leyendo e cuidando el mal que fazen o tienen en la voluntad de fazer los porfiosos de sus malas maestrías, e descobrimiento publicado de sus muchas engañosas maneras que usan para pecar e engañar las mujeres, acordarán la memoria e non despreciarán su fama; ca mucho es cruel quien su fama menosprecia: el Derecho lo dize. E querrán más amar a sí mismos que al pecado, que la ordenada caridad de sí mismo comiença: el Decreto lo dize." (11) ["those of little understanding will not be lost, for on reading and pondering the evil that is done or is intended to be done by those who persist in their wicked arts, and through the published revelation of the many deceitful measures they employ for sinning and for deceiving women, they (i.e., those of little understanding) will bestir their memory and will not disdain their good repute; for very cruel is he who holds his own reputation in low esteem: the Law says so. And they will rather love themselves than sinfulness, for well ordered charity begins with the self: the Decretal says so."] The belief that "well ordered charity begins with the self" is, as we have seen, the very cornerstone of Augustine's system. It is on the power of the mind, of human memory (hence of the efficacy of exemplary discourse) that the two authors disagree.

This judgment voiced by Juan Ruiz would seem to relegate man to the bleak status of an ineducable sinner. Such a negative view concerning the power of human intellection as a means of attaining salvation, moreover, obviously runs counter to Augustine's belief in the constructive nature of human memory. In point of fact, however, the Archpriest does offer us a solution — a remedy for our poorness of memory. For while poorness of human memory does not allow us to interpret empirical reality so as to lead man to Divine reality, according to Juan Ruiz, the "memory of the soul" (charity) can. This is the essential distinction which the Archpriest emphasizes in his prologue by means of parallel syntactic structure:

> es más apropiada la memoria al alma, que es espíritu de Dios criado e perfeto, e bive siempre en Dios. Otrossí dize David: *Anima mea illi vivet: quaerite Dominum et vivet anima vestra.* E non es apropiada al cuerpo umano que dura poco tiempo. E dize Job: *Breves dies hominis sunt.* E otrossí dize: *Homo, natus de muliere; breves dies hominis sunt.* E dize sobre esto David: *Anni nostri sicut aranea mediabuntur, et caetera.* (9)

> [memory is more characteristic of the soul (than of the intellect), which is spirit created by God and is perfect, and lives always in God. Likewise David says: 'To Him my soul shall live ... seek ye the Lord and your soul shall live. And it (memory) is not characteristic of the human body, which endures but a little time.' And Job says: 'The days of a man are short.' And likewise he says: 'Man that is born of a woman is of a few days.' And about this David says: 'Our years shall be considered as a spider (web), et cetera.']

As is evident from the Archpriest's words, he adopts the Augustinian valorization of charity. However, unlike Augustine, who finds great validity in the contemplation of our earthly life as a vehicle for achieving everlasting spiritual life — the constructive power of intellection through recollection — Juan Ruiz is interested in mimimizing the importance of man's earthly life in the way in which Augustine exploits it. He invokes the authority of David and Job in support of his contention. Retrospective remembering and intense self-analysis of the sort advocated by Augustine will not lead all readers to spiritual enlightenment, for few are capable of such intense self-analysis. Only those readers who are already of a certain charitable moral fiber when they come to the text (readers of good will hence of good understanding) will profit in spiritual terms by reading the *Libro,* for only they have the *a priori* capacity to interpret it properly. Thus we see that Juan Ruiz retains one of Augustine's most important premises here. What he is unwilling to do, however, is to accept Augustine's leap of logic, to acknowledge that the *Confessions* itself (or that Augustine) succeeds in creating a universal Christian reader figure by means of the act of reading. While Augustine explicitly claims that he writes a polysemous text (mirroring the polysemy of Scripture), its polysemy exists only within the parameters of possible Christian readings — of readings undertaken with charity. In other words, the inscribed and implied readers are designed to merge in the Augustinian text.

In the *Libro* on the other hand there exists from the beginning to the end of the text a multiplicity of inscribed readers. Diego Catalán writes suggestively of the Archpriest's concern with his avowedly heterogeneous reading public: "tiene bien presente [el Arcipreste] la materialidad del 'libro,' pues desea que 'ande de mano en mano,' 'emprestado' y no 'vendido ni alquilado' (sts. 1629-30). [12] Moreover, Catalán offers a catalogue of some of the inscribed readers specifically mentioned by the Archpriest: "varones" (st. 1628), "amigos," "señores" and "varones" (sts. 1132-35), the "clérigo synple" (st. 1154), the "abogado de rromance" (st. 353), "dueñas" (sts. 114, 122, 947-49). The Archpriest is well aware that these people will each understand and interpret his book "según su particular 'seso,' " as Catalán explains. [13]

---

[12] Diego Catalán, " 'Aunque omne non goste la pera del peral,' " p. 79.
[13] Catalán, p. 79. Other inscribed readers who could be added to this list are: "wise" and "foolish" readers (10); "poets" (12); the "courteous listener" (st. 949), etc.

The multiplicity of interpretations to which his book will be subject is a recurring theme throughout the book, one which Juan Ruiz elaborates particularly in the prologue and in the concluding stanzas. The last four stanzas of the narrative proper are especially revelatory of the reading-theory which he articulates in the prologue and which he espouses throughout the poem:

> Fiz'vos pequeño libro de testo, mas la glosa
> non creo que es chica, ante es bien grand prosa;
> ca sobre cada fabla se entiende otra cosa,
> sin lo que se alega en la razón fermosa.
>
> De la santidad mucha es muy grand licionario,
> mas de juego e de burla es chico breviario;
> por ende fago punto e cierro mi almario:
> séavos chica burla, solaz e letuario.
>
> Señores, hevos servido con poca sabidoría;
> por vos dar solaz a todos, fablévos en juglaría;
> yo un galardón vos pido: que por Dios, en romería,
> digades un paternoster por mí e avemaría.
>
> Era de mill e trezientos e sesenta e ocho años
> fue acabado este libro, por muchos males e daños
> que fazen muchos e muchas a otros con sus engaños,
> e por mostrar a los simples fablas e versos estraños.
>
> (sts. 1631-1634)

> [I have made you a book that is small in terms of text, but the exegesis, I believe, is not brief, rather it is a good big piece of writing; for in respect to each tale something else is to be understood, apart from what is said in the pretty wording.
>
> It is a very big doctrinal book about a great deal of holiness, but it is a small breviary of fun and jokes; so I am making an end and closing my cupboard: may it be for you a brief jest, a delight, and a sweet confection.
>
> Ladies and gentlemen, I have done you service with my scanty learning; to give pleasure to you all, I have addressed you in jocular minstrel fashion; I beg a reward of you: that in the name of God, on a pilgrimage, you say a Lord's Prayer for me and a Hail Mary.

In the year of the Era of Caesar Augustus, one thousand, three hundred and sixty-eight [A.D. 1330], this book was finished, for many evils and wrongs that many men and women do to others with their deceits, and to display to simple people exemplary tales and ingenious verses.]

We see in stanza 1631 the use of the highly charged term "glosa" (exegesis), a word which is normally reserved for explication of the Bible. The suggestion of a scriptural analogue is pursued even further as the Archpriest tells us that the exegesis of his *Libro* is very long by comparison with the poem itself. (He does not offer an exegesis because this is the reader's own task and because each reader will interpret the *Libro* differently.) Moreover, he notes, every tale carries with it a meaning in addition to its literal significance. Again, here too he refuses to offer one explicit interpretation because reading cannot logically afford one. Finally, he affirms that the *Libro* "De la santidad es muy grand licionario" in stanza 1632a ("It is a very big doctrinal book about a great deal of holiness"). In speaking of his text in terms of the Bible, Juan Ruiz recalls Augustine's exploitation of Scriptural exegesis and polysemy as the model for reading the *Confessions*. Yet, as in the prologue, and by sharp contrast with Augustine, the Archpriest insists upon the divergent interpretations (secular as well as sacred) in which his book will necessarily result: "Qualquier omne que l'oya, si bien trobar sopiere, / puede mas añedir e emendar lo que quisiere; / ande, de mano en mano, a quienquier que lo pediere; / como pella las dueñas, tómelo quien podiere" (st. 1629). ["Whoever hears it, if he knows how to compose poetry, may add more to it and emend whatever he wishes to; let it pass from hand to hand to anyone who may request it; as ladies catch a ball, let him catch it who can."]

Hence it will be interpreted by some as an *ars poetica*, as a poetic text to be emulated and perhaps continued. Alternatively, stanza 1634 — the last one of the narrative proper — offers a different hierarchy of possible interpretations. Juan Ruiz confesses there that he wrote the book for two reasons: in order to illustrate human deceptiveness ("muchos males e daños que fazen muchos e muchas a otros con sus engaños"), and "to display to simple people exemplary tales and ingenious verses" ("mostrar a los sinples fablas e versos estraños," [stanza 1634d]). A considerable degree of irony appears to be contained in this last statement of purpose. For surely "simple readers" are not equiped to appreciate the intricacies of "ingenious verses." The difficulty inherent in this somewhat puzzling statement disappears, however, if we recognize the sophisticated, subtle readers (those of good understanding) to be those who go beyond the literal and formal aspects, those who are capable of perceiving the book as a unified whole detailing human frailty, and who rightly understand the "buen amor de Dios." [14]

The disparity of meanings afforded by the *Libro* — ranging from ways of praying to the Lord, to ways of deceiving others, to ways of writing poetry are all acknowledged by the Archpriest, for he realizes that they are all built into his text and that such diversity of interpretation is in fact inescapable.

Indeed, the *Libro* thematizes the problem of interpretation by dramatizing the conflict inherent in the Augustinian paradox. An author cannot prescribe one univocal interpretation, because various readers will interpret a given passage or text variously (according to their individual aprioristic moral state).

For Leo Spitzer, the Archpriest's attitude towards interpretation is, as discussed above, entirely in keeping with the poetic practices of medieval literature — as an expression of the widely-disseminated "world as book" topos: [15]

> Así como el mundo siempre nuevo y en eterna renovación es, sin embargo, solamente la glosa del texto escrito un día por Dios en la Biblia, así también el libro humano,

---

[14] María Rosa Lida de Malkiel, in her review, "Thomas Hart, *La alegoría en el 'Libro de buen amor'*" (*Romance Philology*, 14, 4 [1961] p. 343), voices this view also: st. 1634 "subraya los dos niveles del poema — apresto estético para el lector simple, enseñanza moral práctica para el lector cuerdo." The more standard interpretation of this stanza, however, sees it as being parodic, not intended to be taken seriously. See Zahareas, *The Art of Juan Ruiz*, pp. 174-78. For a different view see Nicolás Emilio Álvarez, "El epílogo del *Libro de buen amor*," *Medieval, Renaissance and Folklore Studies in Honor of John Esten Keller*, ed., Joseph R. Jones (Newark, Del.: Juan de la Cuesta, 1980), pp. 141-50.

[15] See Ernst Robert Curtius, *European Literature and the Latin Middle Ages* (Princeton: Princeton University Press, 1953), pp. 319-23.

> copia del divino, ha de ser mudable en su interpretación: la glosa del lector pertenece también al texto de la obra poética, igual que la vida terrestre de las criaturas todas pertenece al mundo creído por Dios. ("En torno al arte," pp. 122-23)

In order to support his thesis that the *Libro*'s concern with interpretation is standard in medieval literature (a contention which Spitzer voices largely to combat Castro's view that Juan Ruiz offers a radically new and surprisingly "modern" "valoración de lo personal" ["En torno al arte," p. 123]), Spitzer reminds us further that Augustine referred to the world as a "divine poem," [16] and similarly, that this metaphor is found both in the Old and New Testaments ("En torno al arte," p. 123).

The fact that this metaphorical association existed long before Juan Ruiz composed his work is indisputable. However, Juan Ruiz is qualitatively different in his exploitation of this metaphor because he — unlike Augustine, the Bible and other authors who rely on this topos — refuses qua author to prescribe meaning, [17] seeing the hermeneutic activity entirely as a function of the reader.

As such, the *Libro* may — like the *Confessions* — also be seen in figural terms, yet with a fundamental difference. While the Augustinian text offered a figure of human salvation, the *Libro* projects a figure of human plurality and diversity — and inescapably, therefore, of diverse reader-responses.

The basic structure of the *Libro* reflects this reading-theory — a recognition of the fact that imitative literature will not necessarily succeed in converting its readers to one particular interpretation because human memory is weak, and because few men rely on charity, the "memory of the soul," which Juan Ruiz details in his prologue.

---

[16] Spitzer, "En torno al arte," p. 123. Augustine speaks of the world as a "divine poem" in one of his letters (Migne 33, 527). For further discussion of this image, see Leo Spitzer, *Classical and Christian Ideas of World Harmony* (Baltimore: The Johns Hopkins University Press, 1963), p. 29 ff.

[17] María Rosa Lida de Malkiel takes issue with Hart's reading of the *Libro* as a didactic allegory precisely because the Archpriest refuses to prescribe meaning for his work: "tanto los autores de los *Gestos Romanorum* como Berceo y don Juan Manuel glosan sistemáticamente todos o casi todos los términos del texto alegorizado" ("Thomas Hart, *La alegoría*," p. 342).

We have already spoken of the Augustinian progression, a linear development in which the protagonist rejects the values of secular romance (love-quest) for those of "sacred romance" (religious-quest). For the Archpriest, on the other hand, since man is not aided by his avowedly imperfect memory he as protagonist (as the post-lapsarian Adam) must of necessity remain in a perpetual state of alternation between the values of secular and sacred romance, so to speak. [18] This claim is borne out by the fact that the protagonist does not undergo any chronological development or have any indication whatsoever of age attached to him. While not knowing his age we similarly do not know how much time elapses between the beginning and end of the narration. Indeed, rather than being linear, as we would expect it to be, the temporal designations of this autobiography are clearly (and surprisingly) cyclical in nature (suggesting, I would argue, the limitations of human memory). [19] The protagonist pursues thirteen different women — a recurring pattern in which his love is frustrated each time. Moreover, these multiple scenes of (comically exaggerated) failed love serve an emblematic function. While underscoring the comic nature of such fleshly pursuits, they simultaneously stress their universality.

The midpoint sequence in each of the two texts further illuminates the reading-theory advanced by each author. Both protagonists are plagued by lust, which serves as the central theme of their respective midpoints. Both texts focus on the transformation of the protagonist in the context of religious experience. [20] In

---

[18] For a discussion of the dialectic tension between earthly and religious values in the *Libro*, see Wilhelm Kellerman, "Zur Charakteristik des *Libro de buen amor del Arcipreste de Hita*," *Zeitschrift für romanische Philologie*, 67 (1951), 225-54.

[19] Lida de Malkiel, *Two Spanish Masterpieces*, p. 26: "The most salient structural characteristic is the repetition of parallel episodes. The thirteen amorous adventures of the autobiographical novel, very similar to one another in their details and identical in their outcome, each frustrating the poet's desire, illustrate through their repeated failure the didactic thesis which Juan Ruiz explicitly sets forth when he muses on his first defeat."

[20] Juan Ruiz begins his four mountain adventures by recalling St. Paul's *Epistle to the Thessalonians* I, 5:21, "Omnia autem probate: quod bonum est tenete." Similarly, he ends this sequence with a reference to the *Epistle of St. James* I, 17: "Omne datum optimum et omne donum perfectum desursum est, descendens a Patre luminum, apud quem non est transmutatio nec vicissitudinis obumbratio" (sts. 950a and 1043a of the *Libro*).

each case, the particular treatment accorded to this structurally significant moment in the texts mirrors the reading-theory projected by Augustine and Juan Ruiz respectively.

The Augustinian midpoint (discussed above in terms of the emblematic significance of the fig tree) is the point at which the *Confessions* moves from being a representational text to being an imitative one. It is, in other words, the particular moment of Augustine's conversion — as well as being a parable of Christian salvation in general.

Juan Ruiz also conveys the parabolic function of his Everyman figure at the midpoint of his text; however, it does not offer a model to be imitated — it remains representational.

In general, the midpoint is frequently the moment at which the hero of a romance is given a new identity, where his true nature is revealed for the first time. [21] The identity of the hero which is revealed to us at the conclusion of the Doña Endrina episode (which constitutes, roughly speaking, the midpoint sequence of the work, sts. 653-909) is not — as we had been led to expect from the autobiographical "yo" which initiates the episode — that of the Archpriest himself, but rather of Don Melón de la Huerta. Our narrator glosses the function of the Endrina/Melón tale as follows:

> Entiende bien la estoria de la fija del Endrino;
> díxela por te dar ensiemplo, mas non porque a mí avino.
>
> (st. 909a-b)
>
> [Place the right interpretation on my story about the daughter of the Sloe-thorn; I told it in order to give you a parable, and not because it really happened to me.]

What Juan Ruiz does at this point is to transform the narrator-protagonist configuration of the *Libro* in such a way as to redefine the text's status as (fictional) autobiography. The fact that this transformation takes place at the structurally significant midpoint

---

[21] See Michelle A. Freeman, *The Poetics of 'Translatio Studii' and 'Conjoincture': Chrétien de Troyes's 'Cligés'* (Lexington: French Forum, 1979), esp. the chapter entitled "The Midpoint."

of the poem underscores the fact that the *Libro* cannot be read simply as fictive autobiography, but must be viewed as the work of a "devious" author figure who exploits a whole repertoire of narrative perspectives, who is capable of shifting from one to another without forewarning his readers (in this case from a first- to a third-person protagonist), yet who maintains a first-person structure throughout.

It is this sort of elusiveness — not only the ever-changing quality of the narrator-protagonist configuration, but of virtually all aspects of the *Libro* — which has led R. S. Willis to remark that: "the magic of the Archpriest's poetry makes everything protean, fluid, insubstantial: the author's 'yo' is transmuted into the presence of the Book, or dissolves into Don Melón de la Huerta; the hideous fourth *serrana* is metamorphosed lyrically into Alda, 'fermosa, e byen colorada'; the mice of the fable assume the posture of grave *hidalgos;* and even Trotaconventos herself is transformed after her death into Urraca." [22] It is, moreover, precisely this kind of elusiveness which informs all of the *serrana* material sts. 950-71; 972-92; 993-1005; 1006-42) which follows directly after the Doña Endrina episode.

These four lyrico-narrative episodes constitute a closed system of sorts in that they do not refer to any other part of the *Libro*. This fact has traditionally puzzled critics, leading them to judge the *cánticas de serrana* as extraneous works which Juan Ruiz — in his capacity as *juglar* — very likely composed prior to the writing of the *Libro* and which probably formed part of his song-book. [23]

Much has been written about genre and theme in these episodes, yet their function in the work as a whole remains a mystery. That the meaning of the *serrana* episodes and their existence in the *Libro* is still a subject of considerable controversy is reflected by the multiplicity of interpretations given to them. They have been interpreted primarily in terms of the following five divergent categories: as more or less realistic narrations dealing with the *feminae salvaticae* — savage women believed to live in the mountains who were

---

[22] Raymond S. Willis, "Two Trotaconventos," *Romance Philology*, 17 (1963), 362.

[23] Cf. Gybbon-Monypenny, "Autobiography in the *Libro*," p. 69 and his "The Two Versions of the *Libro*," p. 217.

known for their habit of sexually assaulting unsuspecting men; [24] as parodic inversions of the courtly ideals and diction expounded by Don Amor ("Notas," pp. 105-50); as an early manifestation of the *desengaño* motif concerning carnal love ("Towards an Interpretation," pp. 1-10); as metaphorical representations of certain rites of spring; [25] or finally, as an extended example of geographic realism. [26]

One aspect of these episodes which has not been accorded much attention is their structural function with regard to the midpoint sequence, the Doña Endrina narrative.

These four poetic fragments involve a series of permutations of the narrator-protagonist's identity — a series of variations, as it were, on the theme of the mutable narrator-protagonist configuration, which has just been clearly articulated in the preceding tale of love, that of Doña Endrina. These permutations result from the fact that the male protagonist in each of the four lyrico-narrative units has a strikingly different identity (although, as in the Endrina sequence, here too we have a first-person structure sustained throughout all of the rustic encounters). In *serrana* episode I the male figure who is confronted by "La Chata" is identified as an *escudero* (a "squire," st. 961b). In II he is an anonymous *hombre* (a "man"), identified as "sandío" (a "fool" in st. 991i, and as "roín, gaho, envernizo" (a "no-good, leprous-looking, ice-cold man") in st. 992, whom Gadea de Riofrío meets. Of the four, this second episode is the only one in which the traveller is not identified by his vocation — nonetheless, he is not identified as *arcipreste* either. In III the masculine protagonist with whom Menga Llorente engages in conversation is apparently a *pastor* (a "shepherd," st. 994a): "Preguntóme muchas cosas, cuidóse que era pastor" ["She asked me a number of questions, she imagined I was a shepherd."] Since she believes him to be a *pastor,* he takes on the identity of one, producing on the spot a convincing catalogue of pastoral skills and accomplishments from which the

---

[24] Michel Zink, *La Pastourelle. Poésie et folklore au moyen âge* (Paris: Bordas, 1972), pp. 86-103.

[25] James F. Burke, "Juan Ruiz, the *Serranas,* and the Rites of Spring," *Journal of Medieval and Renaissance Studies,* 5 (1575), 13-35.

[26] Rubén Caba, *Por la ruta serrana del Arcipreste* (Madrid: Cenit, 1977).

serrana concludes that he would make a fine husband. Finally, in IV he is a *fidalgo* (st. 1031b). No explanation is given for these changes. Yet the metamorphosis of the protagonist from one identity to the next in the space of four brief episodes presented as first-person narrations is entirely in keeping with the program of permutations of the narrator-protagonist (and of the authorial *yo*) established in the *Libro*.

Further, the protean nature of the protagonist in the *serrana* sequence is underscored by a kind of generic a-symmetry. That is, his identity is disclosed three of the four times (in I, II and IV) in the intercalated lyrics, but once also in the narrative (III). Thus it is not possible to ascribe the changes to a consistent opposition between lyric and narrative voices. [27]

The mutable nature of this narrator-protagonist represents, on the one hand, a remarkable innovation in autobiographical discourse. In addition to its generic implications, however, it fortifies the Archpriest's presentation of himself as a common man, as an Everyman figure — a fundamentally un-self-reflexive individual whose thoughts and impulses tend to be more earth-bound than divine. Hence in contradistinction to Augustine, what occurs in and around the center of the Archpriest's text is not individual conversion, but rather an affirmation of human pluralism (which accords with his reading-theory). [28]

---

[27] For a detailed treatment of the relationship between the lyric and narrative segments of the *serrana* sequence, see R. B. Tate, "Adventures in the Sierra," '*Libro de buen amor*' *Studies*, ed., G. B. Gybbon-Monypenny (London: Tamesis, 1970), pp. 219-29.

[28] See also my "Permutations of the Narrator-Protagonist Configuration: The *Serrana* Episodes of the *Libro de buen amor* in Light of the Doña Endrina Sequence," *Romance Notes*, 22 (1981), 98-101.

IV. THE NARRATOR/PROTAGONIST/AUTHOR CONFIGURATION

Two important recent analyses by André Michalski and Colbert Nepaulsingh interpret the *Libro* as a systematic deformation of the hagiographic paradigm. Michalski further specifies that the Archpriest's poem is an extended parody of Augustine's *Confessions*. Both inquiries yield a number of important insights for *Libro*-studies in general and, in particular, for the purposes of the present reader-oriented investigation. Therefore each study should be treated here in some detail for they both help further to clarify the role of the reader in the *Libro*.

Both investigations are predicated upon the assumption that the protagonist undergoes a kind of linear progression in which he rejects Catholicism, becoming converted instead to the religion of Don Amor. As Michalski puts it: "lo que la obra narra es su conversión de la fe católica a la religión del Amor y su progresión en ella" ("La parodia hagiográfica," p. 64). And as a corollary to this view he remarks that: "Hasta cierto punto creo que se podría decir que el *Libro de buen amor* es un *Bildungsroman*, o novela educacional, en que el protagonista recibe un adoctrinamiento y pasa por una serie de experiencias que ahondan su sabiduría y lo forman" ("La parodia hagiográfica," p. 58).

In contradistinction to Michalski's view I would like to advance the theory that there is in fact no definitive conversion of the protagonist to the religion of Don Amor. Michalski speaks very intelligently and insightfully about the *Libro* as conscious reworking of selected aspects of the Augustinian text (particularly in terms of certain characterological correspondences), however his perception of a linear (rather than cyclical) progression fails to account, among other things, for the remainder of the work after the battle of Flesh and Lent.

The Archpriest as protagonist does indeed make a "confesión pública de su adhesión a don Amor" ("La parodia hagiográfica," p. 58). And in this context Michalski rightly cites as unambiguous proof stanza 1261:

> "Señor, tú me oviste, de pequeño, criado;
> el bien, si algo sé, de ti me fue mostrado;
> de ti fue apercebido, de ti fue castigado;
> en esta santa fiesta sey de mí ospedado."

> [Lord, you brought me up from a child; what is good, if I know anything at all, was taught to me by you; by you I was instructed, and by you I was given admonitions: on this sacred feast day, allow yourself to be my guest.]

The protagonist confesses his devotion to Don Amor at this point, but this passage cannot be invoked in isolation; to do so would considerably distort the text. It is important to note that there are after this declaration of allegiance to Love several key passages which constitute either implicit or explicit professions of the Archpriest's devotion to the Christian God and to the Virgin Mary. To give a few examples of the Christian constant to which the Archpriest adheres after stanza 1261, we have: sts. 1503-04, where the Archpriest claims God as his guide: "mucho de bien me fizo [Garoça] con Dios en limpio amor; / en quanto ella fue biva, *Dios fue mi guiador* [emphasis mine]. / Con mucha oración a Dios por mí rogava; con la su abstinencia mucho me ayudava;" ["The lady accepted me as her true paramour; I was ever her obedient and loyal lover; many a good thing did she do for me, with God's help, in unsullied love; as long as she lived *God was my guide*"]; in the *planctus* for Trotaconventos he repeatedly invokes God (not Don Amor) to intercede on her behalf (sts. 1568, 1570-72, 1575); sts. 1579-1605 treat in an extended manner of "With what arms every Christian should arm himself to vanquish the Devil, the World, and the Flesh"; finally, in explaining "How the Archpriest says we should understand this book of his" (sts. 1626-33) Juan Ruiz again underscores his Christian belief in a wholly unambiguous way, "Porque Santa María, segund que dicho he, / es comienço e fin del bien, *tal es mi fe*" (emphasis mine) ["Because the Holy Virgin, as

I have said, is the beginning and the end of all good, *so I do believe*"]; similarly, what he requests of his reader is not the worship of Don Amor, but of the Christian God, and that they pray to God on behalf of his soul: "yo un galardón vos pido: que por Dios, en romería, / digades un paternoster por mi e avemaría" ["I beg a reward of you: that in the name of God, on a pilgrimage, you say a Lord's Prayer for me and a Hail Mary" (st. 1633)].

To the extent that the Archpriest tries to influence the behavior of his readers, he consistently does so in terms of God (despite the fact that as a sinner he cannot help but be subject to the temptations of the flesh). He does not advocate the religion of Don Amor, but yields to its impulses because of his identity as "the soul that has died with Adam." [1] Moreover, the argument which claims that everything which follows the Archpriest's statement that he is a disciple of Don Amor is intended parodically, similarly breaks down. For, why should we not view it too as parody? After all, the protagonist is as unsuccessful in his amorous pursuits after this confession as he was before. Hence the religion of Love is as false and ineffectual as the commandments detailed by Don Amor beginning in stanza 181. The reader sees from this — as does the protagonist — that the religion espoused by Don Amor is useless, not achieving what it professes. It is a false religion, as any intelligent reader surmises without having to dwell profoundly on its theory and practice. It is, moreover, calculatedly presented as being ludicrous, as are its practitioners. Love between man and woman is presented neither as a potentially ennobling force nor even as a necessity for the propagation of the human race. Rather it is depicted consistently in the deflationary terms of carnal self-indulgence. [2]

The fundamental theme of human frailty evidenced throughout the poem, is in fact the central theme of the Archpriest's lament for Trotaconventos. This sequence is, significantly, cast in highly

---

[1] *Confessions*, Bk. IX, xiii, p. 64; ("animae quae in Adam moritur").

[2] In this connection, see also Gail Phillips, *The Imagery of the 'Libro de buen amor'* (Madison: Hispanic Seminary of Medieval Studies, 1983), pp. 142-49.

This work appeared after my study was already in press. Thus it was not possible to take its numerous interesting observations into account here in a detailed manner.

subjective terms, as Bruce Wardropper notes: "If Charlemagne and Gonzalo Gustios introduced a note of personal loss into the Spanish elegy, Juan Ruiz goes one stage further, in the fourteenth century, by blending his sense of loss with a sense of self-pity." [3]

That the Archpriest sees the procuress' death according to self-interested motives is clearly established by textual detail at the moment when he first announces her death to his readers:

> Assí fue ¡mal pecado! que mi vieja es muerta;
> murió a mí serviendo, lo que me desconuerta;
> non sé cómo lo diga, ca mucha buena puerta
> me fue después cerrada, que ante me era abierta. (st. 1519)

> [It so happened — damnation on it! — that my old retainer died; she died while serving me, which makes me disconsolate; I don't know how to say it, for many a good door which formerly stood open for me was closed to me thereafter.]

From this surprisingly egocentric articulation of the effects of her death for him, the narrator moves on to the traditional invective against Death personified, the great leveller who is hated, feared, cruel, inevitable and, finally, able to strike when it is least expected. He speaks at length of the fear of death experienced by all humans (there is at this point a notable absence of the Christian hope of life everlasting). This nihilistic diatribe underscores his feeling of loss even further.

However, from this traditional subject matter of the *planctus* Juan Ruiz suddenly shifts to a grotesque portrayal not of the festering corpse or the unbearable grief of the bereaved, but instead of their extreme hypocrisy (sts. 1536-42):

> Desque los sus parientes la su muerte barruntan,
> por lo eredar todo a menudo se ayuntan;
> quando por su dolencia al físico preguntan,
> si dize que sanará, todos gelo repuntan.

> Los que son más propincos, hermanos e hermanas,
> non cuidan ver la ora que tangan las campanas;
> más precian la herencia cercanos e cercanas
> que no al parentesco nin a las barbas canas.

---

[3] Bruce W. Wardropper, "Pleberio's Lament for Melibea and the Medieval Elegiac Tradition," *MLN*, 79 (1964), 144.

Desque sale el alma al rico pecador,
déxanle en tierra solo; todos an d'él pavor;
roban todo el algo, primero lo mejor:
el que lieva lo menos tiénese por peor.

Mucho fazen que luego lo vayan a soterrar;
témense que las arcas les an a desferrar,
por oír luenga missa non lo quieren tardar;
de todos sus tesoros danle chico axuar.

Non dan por Dios a pobres, nin cantan sacreficios,
nin dizen oraciones nin cumplen los oficios;
lo más que en esto fazen los herederos novicios
es dar bozes al sordo, mas non otros servicios.

Sotiérranlo de grado, e desque a gracias van,
amidos, tarde o nunca en missa por él están;
por lo que ellos andavan ya fallado lo an:
ellos lievan el algo, el alma lieva Satán.

Si dexa mujer moça, rica o pareciente,
ante de missa dicha otros la an emiente;
o casa con más rico o moço más valiente;
nunca en el trentanario d'él duelo mucho siente.

[As soon as his relatives catch scent of his death, they keep meeting with him so as to inherit everything; when they ask the physician about his illness, if he says the patient will get well they all take him to task for it.

Those who are the closest kin, his brothers and sisters, cannot wait for the hour when the bells will toll; the close relatives, both men and women, have more regard for the inheritance than for his kinship or his white beard.

The minute his soul departs from a wealthy sinner, he is left all alone in the ground; all are afraid of him; they steal his wealth, first of all what is best: the one who gets the least considers himself the worst.

They work hard to get him buried promptly; they are afraid that somebody may break open the locks of their coffers, they don't want to delay by hearing a long funeral Mass: out of all his treasures they give him a very small trousseau.

They do not give to the poor in the name of God, nor do they have Masses sung; nor do they offer up prayers, nor do they attend the required devotions; the most that the neophyte heirs do in this matter is to make outcry to the deaf one, but no other service.

They bury him gladly, and after they have gone to offer thanks, they attend Masses for him grudgingly, late, or never; they have already found what they were looking for: they carry off his property, Satan carries off his soul.

If he leaves a wife who is young, wealthy, or pretty, before the Mass is over other men get ideas about her; she either marries a richer man or a lustier youth; never during the month's mind (30 days of Masses for his soul) does she have much feeling of grief for him.]

By this unexpected, untraditional (and unconditional) condemnation of the survivors, the Archpriest underscores the basic theme of his book once more — i.e., human frailty. It would be difficult to interpret this wholesale devaluation of human motives and comportment as lighthearted parody, an interpretation which is often expressed with regard to the *planctus* in general. [4]

In the next stanza Juan Ruiz surprises us once more, for the focus of this funeral ode now shifts to an explicitly Christian dimension. Stanzas 1554 to 1567 are an extended equation of death with the Devil. In addition, the Archpriest prays to God that He, in His omnipotence, deliver us from death. This attitude towards God's power over death (and over all else as well) is an orthodox one. The declaration of God's omnipotence, on the one hand, obviously diminishes the importance which should be accorded to the Archpriest's declaration in stanza 1261 that he serves the god of Love. On the other hand, the words concerning God's power against the Devil lead us to believe that we have once again re-entered the boundaries of the traditional Christian *planctus*.

No sooner have we done so, however, than Juan Ruiz reorients our generic expectations once more — this time by likening Trotaconventos to the Virgin Mary and by endowing her with the elevated status of a martyr: "Jesucristo compróla / por la su santa

---

[4] E.g., Wardropper, p. 145; Zahareas, *The Art of Juan Ruiz*, pp. 209-17.

sangre e por ella perdonóla" ["Jesus Christ ransomed her with His sacred blood and with it He gave pardon to her," st. 1568 c-d] ... "Cierto en Paraíso estás tú assentada; / con los márteres deves estar acompañada; / siempre en este mundo fuste por Dios martiriada. / ¿Quién te me rebató, vieja por mí lazrada?" ["Surely you are enthroned in Paradise: you must be in the company of the martyrs; you were ceaselessly martyrized in this world, for God's sake. Who snatched you from me, poor old woman, so toil-worn for me?" (st. 1570).]

The identification of Trotaconventos with the Virgin and with sainthood seriously affects the reader, usually leading him to interpret these equivalences as parodic, as blatant and heretical Christian parody. [5]

In this connection and with respect to Augustine's *Confessions,* Michalski has noticed a whole series of suggestive characterological traits which ally Trotaconventos with Monica, Augustine's mother. Of these several parallels he writes: "El planto por Trotaconventos en el *Libro de buen amor* pudo haber sido inspirado en parte por el lamento de San Agustín a la muerte de un amigo suyo anónimo, y en parte por el elogio que hace de su madre, Santa Mónica, a la muerte de ésta. En el caso de San Agustín, es obvio que el papel de 'medianera de la gracia divina' lo desempeñó Santa Mónica, quien, además de ser una devotísima 'trotaconventos' (en el sentido loable, no irónico de la palabra), fue una incansable casamentera que trató de casarlo cristianamente para apartarle de la lujuria. La muerte repentina de Trotaconventos (como la de Santa Mónica), el amor entrañable — filial — que siente por ella el Arcipreste, y el elogio fúnebre que hace de ella, he aquí tres elementos que por su seriedad se salen del tono en general jocoso del *Libro de buen amor,* y su presencia en él se explican por la fuente que le sirvió de inspiración" ("La parodia hagiográfica," p. 65).

Michalski's observations are fascinating as well as pointing to a real resource for the medieval reader, who saw them no doubt

---

[5] See in this context A. D. Deyermond, "Some Aspects of Parody in the *Libro de buen amor*," '*Libro de buen amor*' *Studies,* pp. 53-77.

as part of a program of Augustinian resonances exploited by Juan Ruiz in the forging of his own text, in his re-writing of Augustine.

Though he does not elaborate the point, Michalski explains in a footnote that: "aún es posible que es en el llanto del joven Agustín que debamos buscar el origen de la imprecación a la muerte del Arcipreste" ("La parodia hagiográfica," p. 65 n.). Indeed, both the friend's death and that of Monica may be seen to figure here in the Archpriest's expression of grief at the death of Trotaconventos. The death of Augustine's friend in Book IV of the *Confessions* — before his conversion to Christianity — is a time of unrelieved sorrow and bitterness for the survivor. In narrating this memory from the time of writing, Augustine specifically juxtaposes his unenlightened (pre-Christian) state, which offered him no solace at the time of the friend's death:

> ecce cor meum, deus meus, ecce intus; vide, quia memini, spes mea (164)... mirabar enim ceteros mortales vivere, quia ille, quem quasi non moriturum dilexeram, mortuus erat; et me magis, quia ille alter eram, vivere illo mortuo mirabar (166)... non enim tu eras, sed vanum phantasma et error meus erat deus meus. (168)

> [My heart (present of the time of writing) lies before you, O my God. Look deep within. See these memories of mine, for you are my hope... (shift back to the time of the narrative). I wondered that other men should live when he was dead, for I had loved him as though he would never die. Still more I wondered that he should die and I remain alive, for I was his second self... The god I worshipped was my own delusion, and if I tried to find in it a place to rest my burden, there was nothing there to uphold it (77-78).]

In contradistinction to this total sense of loss and disorientation at the time of the friend's death, the death of Monica has an appreciably different effect on Augustine. While he was profoundly saddened by her death (Book IX), his fervent religious belief prevails in assuaging his grief: "... neque enim decere arbitrabamur funus illud questibus lacrimosis gemitibusque celebrare, quia his pleurumque solet deplorari quaedam miseria morientium aut quasi omnimodo extinctio. at illa nec misere moriebatur nec omnino moriebatur. hoc et documentis morum eius et fide non ficta rationibusque certis tenebamus" (58). ["... we did not think it right to mark my mother's death with weeping and moaning, because such lamentations are the usual accompaniment of death when it is thought of as a state of misery or as total extinction. But she had not died in misery, nor had she wholly died. Of this we were certain, both because we know what a holy life she had led and also because our faith was real and we had sure reasons not to doubt it" (200).]

The difference between Augustine's response to Monica's death and the Archpriest's to that of his procuress is clear. The *planctus* delivered by Juan Ruiz is the lament of a secular man who — like Augustine at the death of his anonymous friend — is too closely tied to his earthly existence. By the characterological reminiscences which Juan Ruiz selectively borrows from Augustine he represents Monica's death, casting himself into the role of the unconverted Augustine. In generating for his readers an analogy between Trotaconventos, the Virgin and a martyr, the Archpriest qua author is being implicitly didactic — offering an *exemplum ex negativo* of a man who is not totally converted to the religious beliefs of Christianity, just as he is not totally committed to that of Don Amor (as witnessed by his invocations to the Christian God. e.g., sts. 1554-67). True conversion involves renunciation, and the protagonist is incapable of renouncing his fleshly impulses.

Thus it will be seen that Juan Ruiz's treatment of Trotaconventos does not constitute a parodic inversion of Monica, but rather a re-writing of the Augustinian subtext in order to produce an emblem of human frailty.

By the same token, Michalski's conceptualization of Don Amor and Doña Venus as inversions of St. Ambrose and the Virgin in the *Confessions* fails to acknowledge the complexity of the Archpriest's poem. For at the *Libro*'s midpoint Juan Ruiz is not, as we have seen, converted to the religion of Love. Instead the protagonist who is revealed to us in the *planctus* for Trotaconventos — as in the Doña Endrina episode and the *serranas* — is poor of memory (in Augustinian terms), corruptible, comical, yet also religious. We recall, for example, that as soon as the protagonist escaped from the very un-courtly mountain wenches, he prayed to the Virgin, offering in her honor two poetic compositions on the theme of Christ's Passion (sts. 1046-58; 1059-66). The contrast between this devotional poetry and the grotesque rustic encounters could not be greater. Yet this contrast is intended as an implicit — but bold — commentary on human nature; to call the readers' attention to the fundamental duality of man: on the one hand, the desires of the flesh; on the other, the desire to serve God.

Significantly, this bivalence of human impulses is clearly articulated by Augustine in the opening lines of the *Confessions*:

> laudare te vult homo, aliqua portio creaturae tuae, et homo circumferens mortalitatem suam, circumferens testimonium peccati sui et testimonium, quia superbis resistis: et tamen laudare te vult homo, aliqua portio creaturae tuae. (2)

> [Man is one of your creatures, Lord, and his instinct is to praise you. He bears about him the mark of death, the sign of his own sin, to remind him that you thwart the proud. But still, since he is part of your creation, he wishes to praise you (21).]

By contrast with Augustine, who wishes to instruct the reader to transform the two natures into one, Juan Ruiz sees this enterprise as an impossibility — choosing instead, therefore, to exemplify the duality, to poeticize it, by composing his book according to cyclical (alternating) structures, which become increasingly evident in the second half of his text.

The very end of the *planctus* offers further proof of this alternation between the values of the spirit and those of the flesh. Having spoken first of Death as the all-powerful leveller, moving thereafter to a catalogue of forms of human hypocrisy (the comportment of the survivors of the deceased), subsequently commending himself to God, the Omnipotent, to deliver us from Death, finally, raising Trotaconventos to the status of a martyr — he ends by yet another unexpected (and deflationary) reversal. Namely, recalling the first image he implemented in order to rail against the evils of Death (Death the leveller), the Archpriest ends his lament by casting Trotaconventos herself in the role of "leveller":

Dueñas, non me rebtedes nin me llamedes neçuelo,
que si a vos serviera, avríades d'ella duelo;
lloraríades por ella, por su sotil anzuelo:
que *quantas seguía tantas ivan por el suelo.* (st. 1573) [6]

[Ladies, do not taunt me nor call me a trifle foolish, for if she had served you, you too would mourn her; you would weep for her and for her craftily baited hook: *every lady whom she went in pursuit of was dragged to the ground.*]

Stanzas 1579-1605 ("De quáles armas se deve armar todo cristiano para vencer el Diablo, el Mundo e la Carne" ["With what arms every Christian should arm himself to vanquish the Devil, the World and the Flesh"]), as this ascetic rubric suggests, focus our attention once again on religious matters. The alternation or cyclical rhythm resumes directly thereafter with a catalogue of the attributes which little women have (sts. 1606-17), and with the last episode of the narrative proper — that of Don Furón (sts. 1618-25).

The meaning produced by this cyclical framework is, in effect, that human history (on the individual level) repeats itself. Our memory is short and imperfect, as the Archpriest emphatically states in the prologue. Therefore, one person cannot profit from the experience or admonitions (oral or written) of another. We know that earthly love, like earthly life, is transitory. Nonetheless, the flesh is weak — so that once the epic battle of Lady Lent and Lord Meatseason culminates on Easter Sunday, it is not Christ but rather Sir Love who (along with Lord Meatseason) emerges as the ruler of Earth, and whose victory is celebrated in a triumphal procession (palm branches and all). Next year, we realize, the scene and its outcome will be precisely the same. Indeed, the seemingly unintegrated Cuaresma/Carnal episode may be said to function emblematically — as a representation of the human psyche (the perpetual psychomaquia resulting from its duality).

The sequence of the canonical hours (sts. 372-87) and the poem which plays on the *double entendre* of "cruz" (both the Cross of Christ's Passion and the common female name, specifically the

---

[6] Emphasis mine.

name of the baker girl whom he pursued, sts. 115-21) similarly function to illustrate the dual aspect of man's nature, physical and spiritual love.[7] For the protagonist is the post-lapsarian sinner who is shaded by the pear-tree. In both instances it is not religion per se which is being parodied, but rather man's distortion of it. In both cases also, we see a failed lover and a failed Christian who is at the same time a brilliant poet.

Don Amor himself reveals the cyclical, oscillating nature of man in his anthropomorphic presentation of the seasons (sts. 1271-1300). The first of the four closely-related versions of the same riddle in this lengthy sequence (which, he later explains, represent the four seasons of the year), reads as follows:

> Tres cavalleros comían, todos a un tablero,
> assentados al fuego, cada uno señero;
> non se alcançarían con un luengo madero
> e non cabría entre ellos un canto de dinero. (st. 1271)

> [Three knights were eating at a single table, seated by the fire, each one by himself; they could not have reached each other with a long pole, and between them the edge of a coin could not have fitted.]

In glossing this enigma along with the other three, Don Amor reveals that these are:

> quatro temporadas del año del espera;
> los omnes son los meses, cosa es verdadera;
> andan e non se alcançan, atiéndense en ribera. (1300)

> [the four seasons of the year of the celestial sphere; the men are the months, this is the truth; they advance but they do not overtake each other, they meet at their borders.]

While the depiction of the months as men is standard in medieval iconography,[8] to my knowledge, the riddle structure by which

---

[7] In this context, see James Burke's excellent study, "Love's Double Cross: Language Play as Structure in the *Libro de buen amor*," *University of Toronto Quarterly*, 43 (1974), 231-62.

[8] See James C. Webster, *The Labors of the Months in Antique and Medieval Art* (Princeton: Princeton University Press, 1938), and Erik Dal,

Juan Ruiz presents the months is unique. It is, moreover, in keeping with his belief in the limits of exemplary discourse.[9] That is, the men do not profit from one another — they are each self-contained microcosms, so to speak.

The structural oscillation of the *Libro* (like the protagonist's oscillation between the poles of secular and sacred romance) is designed to mirror the relentlessly oscillating nature of the human psyche in general. And it is for this reason that the Archpriest's poem lacks "poetic closure" (a definitive ending) as he explicitly tells us:

> Porque Santa María, segund que dicho he,
> es comienço e fin del bien, tal es mi fe,
> fiz'le quatro cantares, e con tanto faré
> punto a mi librete, mas non lo cerraré. (st. 1626) . . .
>
> Qualquier omne que l'oya, si bien trobar sopiere,
> puede más añedir e emendar lo que quisiere; (st. 1629a-b)
>
> [Because the Holy Virgin is, as I have said, the beginning and end of all good, so I do believe, I composed four songs for her, and thereupon I shall put an end to my book, but I shall not close it.
>
> Whoever hears it, if he knows how to compose poetry, may add more or emend whatever he wishes to . . .]

Moreover, as Nepaulsingh astutely argues, there is no clear stopping point or precise, unambiguous beginning to the *Libro* either:

> Although the "Gozos" [sts. 20-43; 1635-49] form a rather decisive beginning and end to the book, it is aesthetically important to respect the Archpriest's desire not to be confined to a single beginning and a single end ("Structure," p. 67) . . . The aesthetic function of the introductory and

---

The Ages of Man and the Months of the Year: Poetry, Prose and Pictures Outlining the "Douze mois figurées" Motif Mainly Found in Shepherds Calendars and in Livres d'Heures (14th to 17th Century) (Copenhagen: Munksgaard, 1980).

[9] Cf. Eduardo Forastieri Braschi's "La descripción de los meses en el Libro de buen amor," *Revista de Filología Española*, 55 (1972), 213-32, also. He does not explain the riddles.

> terminatory material is to lend an air of indecisive formlessness to the entire work by detracting, but at the same time highlighting the structure of the more decisive unit ("Structure," p. 68).

For Nepaulsingh, the "decisive unit" is the juxtaposition of opposites whereby, for example, "the triumph of Don Amor is intended as a deliberate contrast to the Passion of Jesus Christ" ("Structure," p. 69). The *Libro* functions, in his view, as a negative example in which the Archpriest is an avatar of the Devil ("Structure," p. 72).

Two interrelated points should be made in this regard. First, Nepaulsingh, investigating the *Libro* from a different angle than the present study — namely, the optic of rhetoric — discerns a type of bivalent structuring by Juan Ruiz which accords with the cyclical framework discussed above (although he interprets its meaning in a radically different way):

> *Exsuperatio,* stated briefly, is overstatement to the point of absurdity; its function is to create suspicion by its very excesses, thus exposing the invalidity of the thing exaggerated. The *Libro de buen amor* is a moralizing Christian work because it contains, between brief affirmations of its Christian morality, a lengthy and absurd art of love. Because he dwells at such absurd length on "loco amor" the Archpriest is affirming the truth of his belief in the "buen amor" that is the beginning and end of all good works like his ("Structure," p. 72).

My own interpretation of the narrator clearly differs from Nepaulsingh's view of him as devil. Granted, he is sinful, as he himself admits. Yet to speak of this narrator as a "devil" — particularly given the fact that he does not become converted to the religion of Don Amor — is an extreme view. Such a conception of the Archpriest as devil is, moreover, inconsistent with Nepaulsingh's own insightful observation, based on rhetorical norms, that the *Libro* is a fundamentally didactic Christian work. How can the Archpriest simultaneously be the embodiment of sin (a parody of Christian values) and a Christian exemplar (a spokesman for these values)?

The answer lies in the necessary distinction which must be made between protagonist, narrator, and author figure. The Archpriest both as protagonist and as narrator is — as he openly states in stanza 76, a sinner, a condition which will remain constant throughout the poem, since he is writing from the present of the time of writing. However, beyond these two levels of narration there is a third which must be taken into account, that of the silent author figure who structures his work in such a way that the implied reader — he who is of good understanding — will perceive the didactic structure of the work (which accords with Nepaulsingh's insight on Juan Ruiz's use of *exsuperatio*). [10]

Logically, the largely implicit (yet unmistakable) nature of the *Libro*'s didacticism is the only possible mode of expression available to the Archpriest qua author — given his particular reading-theory, his belief that people cannot be converted through the act of reading. For, to harangue his readers with didacticism, while not necessarily affecting their behavior, would surely detract from his poetic creation.

Wise readers are — as they were in the Augustinian system — those who read with Christian charity. As a result, the *Libro* is not designed, as many interpreters believe, as a travesty of Christian doctrine and ceremony. That the text is frequently parodic is undeniable. However, the object of this parody is man himself. [11] In every case where the Christian value system participates in some form of parody — the episode of Cruz, the baker girl, the canonical hours, the battle of Lent and Flesh, etc. — it serves to underscore the short-comings of the fallen Everyman, the narrator-protagonist whose thoughts are, regrettably, more earthbound than divine.

It is, in brief, the all-important relationship of the author figure to his narrator-protagonist which makes manifest Juan Ruiz's exploitation of parody (sacred as well as secular) throughout the *Libro*.

---

[10] This author figure is analogous in function to the one who exists in the sixteenth-century paradigm of confessional literature — *Lazarillo de Tormes,* as defined by Stephen Gilman in his important study, "The Death of Lazarillo de Tormes," *PMLA,* 81 (1966), 149-66.

[11] See Deyermond, "Some Aspects of Parody in the *Libro de buen amor.*"

V. PARABLES OF INTERPRETATION

The Archpriest's fundamental concern with the problematics of interpretive reading can be traced in many of his episodes. The dispute between the Greeks and Romans (sts. 44-70) and the conflicting interpretations of the astrologers (sts. 123-65) are particularly illuminating examples. Moreover, they should be studied in tandem because of their identical function as models of reading.

The episode of the Greeks and Romans (sts. 44-70) is the first *exemplum* in the *Libro* and as such it occupies a privileged position in the Archpriest's hermeneutic system. Zahareas sees stanzas 44-70 as the very "kernel of the *Libro*'s structure; the findings concerning theme and form should apply for the entire *Libro*" (*The Art of Juan Ruiz*, p. 43). He places importance on this passage because it offers the reader clues as to how the text as a whole asks to be interpreted. By contrast, he plays down the function of the prose prologue in orienting the reader — viewing it instead in rhetorical and artistic terms (*The Art of Juan Ruiz*, pp. 21-24). Nonetheless, the parable of the Greeks and Romans, as well as that of the astrologers, accord in theme with the prologue. These episodes offer fictional illustrations of what the Archpriest in his prose establishes discursively.

Two principal schools of thought exist regarding the meaning produced by the parable of the Greek sage and the Roman ruffian who misinterpret each other's sign language: the first view finds both contestants to be wrong — the Greek having interpreted the Roman's gestures as religious wisdom and the Roman having interpreted his opponent's signals as threats of physical violence. From the outcome of this dispute (a double misunderstanding by sage and dullard alike), numerous critics conclude that the reader of the *Libro* should choose whichever of the two ostensibly correct (but in reality wrong) interpretations seems right to him. This is the basic view of Spitzer and Zahareas; however, Spitzer assigns an additional, broader didactic sense to his parable as well:

> Los dos contrincantes... simbolizan la verdad trascendente a toda aplicación moral práctica ('Non ha mala palabra, si non es a mal tenida') de que Dios, que ha dado a los hombres (palabras y) gestos para que se entiendan unos a otros, lleva a cabo por encima de los designios de los hombres y a pesar, por decirlo así, de sus equivocaciones... ("En torno al arte," p. 124)

The second basic interpretation of this tale chooses either the Greek or the Roman error as being the preferred (more correct) one. The Greek sage is most often chosen as the preferable interpreter, as Lida de Malkiel explains. Focusing on the sign itself in this dispute, she affirms that: "all its [the sign's] meanings are admissible, but not all are equally valuable; the vulgar meaning which the knave chooses in accordance with his knavery is inferior to the theological meaning which the doctor chooses in accordance with his wisdom and learning (*Two Spanish Masterpieces*, p. 32). Nevertheless, of course, the *sabio*'s learning and wisdom are proved useless, since he fails to comprehend the simple message communicated by the knave. Not to mention, as Deyermond points out, that the Roman gets what he wants (namely the laws) whereas the Greek fails to achieve his goal (i.e., keeping the laws from the Romans).[1]

Stanza 64 immediately follows the story and it is prescribed by the Archpriest as an interpretive tool to his reader:

> Por esto dize la pastraña de la vieja fardida:
> 'non ha mala palabra si non es a mal tenida.'
> Verás que bien es dicha si bien es entendida:
> entiende bien mi libro e avrás dueña garrida.

---

[1] A. D. Deyermond, "The Greeks, the Romans, the Astrologers and the Meaning of the *Libro de buen amor*," *Romance Notes*, 5 (1963), 89-90. See also Sara Sturm, "The Greeks and the Romans: The Archpriest's Warning to his Reader," *Romance Notes*, 10 (1968-9), 404-12.

[This is why the proverb of the shrewd old woman says: 'No word is bad if you don't take it badly.' You will see that my word is well said if it is well understood: understand my book well and you will have a lovely lady.]

Three stanzas later the Archpriest reiterates this idea while at the same time making it more explicit. Acknowledging the relativity of interpretation which this text (like any other) will provoke, he states:

> En general a todos fabla la escritura;
> los cuerdos, con buen seso, entendrán la cordura;
> los mancebos livianos guárdense de locura:
> escoja lo mejor el de buena ventura.
>
> Las de buen amor son razones encobiertas;
> trabaja do fallares las sus señales ciertas;
> si la razón entiendes o en el seso aciertas,
> non dirás mal del libro que agora rehiertas. (sts. 67-68)

[The text speaks to everyone in general; people of good sense will discern its wisdom; as for frivolous young people, let them refrain from folly: let him who is fortunate select the better side.

The utterances of good love are veiled: strive to find their true meanings; if you understand the meaning of what is said or hit upon the sense, you will not speak ill of the book which you now censure.]

Thus what Juan Ruiz does here, as he did in the prologue, is to acknowledge the Augustinian belief that "evil is in the eye of the beholder," so to speak, the relativity of reader response which is contingent upon the moral status of the reading subject.

The theme of conflicting interpretations serves also as the focal point of the *exemplum* of the astrologers (sts. 123-65). At first glance, this second *exemplum* seems to signify the very opposite of the first. For whereas both the Greek and the Roman were wrong in their respective interpretations, each of the five seers is shown to have given an accurate prediction concerning the manner of death which would befall King Alcáraz's son. The element which these two narratives have in common is, as Deyermond insightfully suggests, the intentional polysemy of the Archpriest's text:

> In the first story, we are shown two conflicting interpretations, both of them wrong; in the second, five conflicting interpretations, all of them right. The Archpriest certainly warns us often enough not to misunderstand him (a common protective device in medieval authors), but in the light of these two *exempla* it is hard to accept the view that he is here inviting us to seek a single correct meaning for the *Libro* as a whole ("The Greeks, the Romans," p. 91).

Such a view of the *Libro*'s intended polysemy is entirely in keeping with the advice of the prologue, and once again, may be seen to originate in Augustinian reading-theory. As Augustine explains at length in the last four books of the *Confessions,* many possible correct interpretations exist. However, while the multiplicity of correct interpretations envisaged by Augustine are all strongly Christian in orientation, Juan Ruiz makes a further distinction in his own theory of reading. As we have seen him do before, here too he explicitly comments on (1) the fact that any given text is necessarily polysemous because its readership is comprised of a heterogeneous group of reading subjects, and its corollary (2) namely, the logical fact that, therefore, an author should not attempt (or pretend) to be able to limit interpretation of his text to one prescribed interpretation. Furthermore, Juan Ruiz logically implies that if an author attempts such prescription of interpretation, he will not necessarily convince his readers that it is the true interpretation. For this reason, he calculatedly refrains from prescribing one interpretation (or even a delimited number of exclusive interpretations) for the *Libro*.

Extrapolating from the *exemplum* of the five correct astrological interpretations to a broader framework for the text as a whole, several scholars have concluded that the Archpriest displays a belief in the influence of the stars on the lives of men. Since all five predictions are true, they reason, he must be valorizing the power of astrology, which was ranked among the most serious of scientific disciplines by the medieval mind. Foremost among this critical group are Roger Walker and Anthony Zahareas.

In a comparative study of the *Libro* and the *Caballero Zifar*, Walker finds that the Archpriest is interested in illustrating the truthfulness of astrological data: "Although the Archpriest admits that it is possible (with extreme difficulty and with a great deal of divine co-operation) to overcome one's predestined character, his main stress is on the power of one's horoscope." [2] Walker explains what he sees as the Archpriest's acknowledgment of predestination largely as part of a pattern of (parodic) reversals of elements adopted from the *Zifar*.

Zahareas, on the other hand, views the Archpriest's foregrounding of astrology as an opportunity to dramatize the traditional medieval debate between determinism and free will, a debate which, as he reminds us, has its origins in Augustine ("The Stars," p. 86). According to his reading of astrology in the *Libro*, "while others stress man's free will, Juan Ruiz stresses man's impotence" ("The Stars," p. 88). As with virtually all aspects of the *Libro*, other critics derive the opposite lesson from the treatment accorded to astrology. Among this latter group are R. S. Willis, Pierre Ullman and Otis Green, all of whom see the example of astrology as yielding a very orthodox view of free will. Ullman affirms, for example, that "Juan Ruiz clearly shows that man does indeed have free will, given to him by God if he is willing to attain it through prayer." [3]

What is immediately apparent from these diametrically opposing scholarly opinions is the degree of ambivalence which the Archpriest builds into his remarks on astrology qua narrator-protagonist. This calculatedly bivalent attitude is very similar to that encountered in the lament for Trotaconventos, discussed above. On the one hand, we see the protagonist oscillating between pagan and Christian values. On the other, we see the author once again recalling a particular episode taken from the *Confessions*.

Having in his youth discovered and embraced for a time the philosophy of the Manichees, Augustine devoted himself to the study of the stars. Yet, having dwelt upon their possible significance,

---

[2] Roger M. Walker, "Juan Ruiz's Defense of Love," *MLN*, 89 (1969), 297.

[3] See Pierre Ullman, "Stanzas 140-150 of the *Libro de buen amor*," *PMLA*, 79 (1964), 203, n. 13.

he concludes that they are subsumed under God's power, elements which He created and controls. From the perspective of the time of writing, Augustine explains his rejection of astrology as an inherently valuable science:

> At tu, amor meus, in quem deficio, ut fortis sim, nec ista corpora es, quae videmus quamquam in caelo, nec ea, quae non videmus ibi, quia tu ista condidisti nec in summis tuis conditionibus habes. (116, 118)

> [You, O God whom I love and on whom I lean in weakness so that I may be strong, you are not the sun and the moon and the stars, even though we see these bodies in the heavens; nor are you those other bodies which we do not see in the sky, for you created them, and in your reckoning, they are not even among the greatest of your works. (61)]

In contradistinction to this attitude and, as with the *planctus* for Trotaconventos, the battle between Cuaresma and Carnal, his attitude towards Don Amor, etc. — Juan Ruiz the character is imperfect, the sinner who is unable to reject his earthly perspective in order to gain a clearer divine perspective.

Finally, Juan Ruiz qua author is viewed by many interpreters as valorizing the influence of astrology because he offers an explanation of his own character in strictly astrological terms — specifically, that he was born under the sign of Venus (sts. 152-54):

> muchos nacen en Venus, que lo más de su vida
> es amar las mugeres, nunca se les olvida;
> trabajan e afanan mucho sin medida,
> e los más non recabdan la cosa más querida.
>
> En este signo atal creo que yo nací:
> siempre puné en servir dueñas que conocí;
> el bien que me fezieron non lo desagradecí;
> a muchas serví mucho, que nada acabecí.
>
> Comoquier que he provado mi signo ser atal:
> en servir a las dueñas punar e non en ál;
> pero aunque non goste la pera del peral,
> en estar a la sombra es plazer comunal.

> [many are born when Venus rules their astral sign, so the greater part of their life consists in loving women, their minds are never off it; they work hard and toil greatly, without stint, and most of them do not obtain the thing that is most dear to them.
>
> Under this very sign I believe that I was born: I have always striven to serve the ladies I have known; the good things they have done me I never was ungrateful for; many ladies have I done much service to, yet nothing have I accomplished.
>
> Although I have proven that my natal destiny was this: to put my efforts into serving (...) ladies and into nothing else (i.e., and never to succeed in possessing them); nevertheless, although one may not taste the pear of the pear tree, just being in its shade is a pleasure fit for everyone.]

As these stanzas reveal, however, the Archpriest offers not a valorization but rather a deflation of the power of the stars. These three quatrains are all variations of the same theme, namely, that although the Archpriest was born under the influence of Venus — hence his unrelenting amorous pursuits — he is a total failure in love. So that the discerning reader does not miss the point either of his views on astrology or of the protagonist as a consistent failure in terms of love, the same message is reiterated three times in the brief span of these three consecutive quatrains.

This unambiguous assertion by the Archpriest is of prime importance for two reasons. First, it underlies once again the comicality of the blundering protagonist, whose repeated attempts and failures signal to the reader that he is to function as a negative *exemplum* of the human conduct which is being advocated by the Archpriest as author. Secondly, the repeated confirmation of the protagonist's series of failures — without exception — informs the reader that his relationship with Doña Garoça is, like all the others, not a success in terms of physical love. The implications of this revelation are highly significant, because it emphasizes the fact that the *Libro* cannot be read as an art of love, as the triumph of Don Amor, or of the Archpriest's conversion to the religion of love. Rather, it is intended as a further instance of the protagonist's oscillation between the values of carnal and spiritual love, the bivalence by which the author defines the human condition in the person of his narrator-protagonist.

A shift appears to occur in the course of the Garoça episode whereby the Archpriest seems to have altered his perspective, to have become "spiritually enlightened" to some extent. Stanza 1501 reveals to the reader that although the protagonist had initially sought a physical relationship, the nun did not accede to his request:

> Pero que sea errança contra Nuestro Señor
> el pecado de monja a omne doñeador,
> ¡ay Dios! ¡e yo lo fuesse aqueste pecador
> que feziesse penitencia d'este fecho error!
>
> [Although sinning with a nun is for the wooer an offense against God, O God, how I wish I were that sinner, to do penance for this sin after it was consummated!]

Having respected her wish to define their relationship in terms of "limpio amor" (in which the Archpriest tells us, "Dios fue mi guiador," st. 1503), he seems to have finally learned to appreciate this higher form of spiritual (rather than carnal) human love:

> Con mucha oración a Dios por mí rogava;
> con la su abstinencia mucho me ayudava,
> la su vida muy limpia en Dios se deleitava;
> en locura del mundo nunca se trabajava. (1504)
>
> [With many a supplication she prayed to God for me; by her abstinence she aided me greatly; her immaculate life found delight in God; she never busied herself with the mad sensuality of this world.]

Greatly afflicted by Garoça's sudden and unexpected death, Juan Ruiz composes, as he tells us, a dirge in her honor. Interestingly, he explains to us that this composition was not written very artfully because he was so distracted by his grief. This is the only time in the *Libro* when the Archpriest as poet claims to have not written a skillful composition: "Con el mucho quebranto fize aquesta endecha; / con pesar e tristeza non fue tan sotil fecha" (st. 1507a-b). ["In my great affliction I composed this dirge; because of grief and sorrow it was not done very skillfully."] As such, it contrasts sharply with his intermittent but insistent boastings of poetic prowess.

This great sadness which is so strong as to affect his abilities as poet leads the reader to assume that the protagonist has finally learned the virtue of spiritual human love, that he has attained a higher meaning in human relationships, leading us further to expect that he will no longer seek physical liaisons. Indeed, the Archpriest's comment at the Moorish girl's refusal to become involved with him also presents a sadder but wiser protagonist (st. 1508):

> Por olvidar la coita, tristeza e pesar,
> rogué a la mi vieja que me quisiesse casar;
> fabló con una mora, non la quiso escuchar:
> ella fizo buen seso; yo fiz' mucho cantar.

> [To forget my distress, sorrow, and grief, I begged my old retainer to try to arrange a liaison for me; she spoke to a Moorish girl, who refused to listen to her: the girl did a wise thing; as for me, I composed a number of songs.]

With the death of Trotaconventos which follows directly after (sts. 1520-78) and the speech (sts. 1579-1605) on "With what arms every Christian should arm himself to vanquish the Devil, the World, and the Flesh," the reader retains the impression that the Archpriest has finally achieved a kind of superior wisdom regarding the life of the flesh and the superiority of the spirit. Nonetheless, as soon as this passage on the arms and objectives of the Church militant is concluded, what follows is a catalogue of the laudable attributes of little women (sts. 1606-17) and, thereafter, an unanticipated return, from the perspective of the reader, to his fleshly pursuits. He instructs his new go-between, Furón, as follows: "Hurón, amigo, catadme nueva funda" (st. 1623a) ["Ferret, my friend, find me a new mopsy."]

Narration of the unsuccessful cycle of amorous quests ends here, but Juan Ruiz shows no signs of giving up the hunt. Although his "grand menester" (1622d) is not assuaged by the lady to whom Furón delivers the message (because the go-between himself becomes her lover), the Archpriest gives no evidence of any inclination to renounce his perpetual, although unfulfilled, love-quest. Hence, as with all the other narrative episodes, that of Garoça (and the two attempted liaisons which fail thereafer) participates in the oscillating pattern which defines man's dual nature, his struggle between the poles of the flesh and the spirit. It is the bivalence which can be transformed into a univocal vision only by means of true conversion.

In addition, it is interesting — and aesthetically disturbing — that Garoça (the only Christian character in the entire *Libro* who is not corruptible) is in fact presented in the same vein of universal human frailty and sinfulness which the Archpriest qua author has projected with reference to all the other characters of his book (except for the Moorish girl, vv. 1508-12). For having just praised Garoça's abstinence and its beneficial effects on the Archpriest, he surprises the reader by commenting that:

> Para tales amores son las religiosas,
> para rogar a Dios con obras piadosas,
> que para amor del mundo mucho son peligrosas,
> e son muy escuseras, perezosas, mintirosas. (1505)

> [Nuns are (made) for love like this (i.e. un-physical affairs), for praying to God, while doing pious works, since they are very risky for earthly, sensual love, and they are very furtive, laggard, and untruthful.]

By this off-hand remark, the Archpriest addresses himself to the hypocrisy of nuns. The remark strikes a discordant note, coming as it does directly after and immediately before words of high praise for Garoça's chastity and devotion to God.[4] Indeed, by not distinguishing her from the "religiosas" about whom he generalizes in stanza 1505, we do not quite know what to think of Garoça herself. Once again, human duality (or duplicity) is suggested, and the reader is left to make of it what he will, according to his particular understanding.

---

[4] Of course the corruptibility of nuns and priests in general is a theme which pervades the *Libro,* and which finds its most striking expression in sts. 1235-62 — the enthusiastic reception which multitudes of nuns and priests of different orders give to the god of Love on Easter Sunday.

Confession without Conversion

The digression concerning the sacrament of Penance (sts. 1128-72) similarly affords a multiplicity of possible interpretations as a result of the Archpriest's intentionally polysemous structuring of his text. This narrative has been interpreted by modern scholars in two basic ways. The first interpretation, as represented by Lecoy and Lida de Malkiel, sees this discourse as a serious exposition of Church doctrine. More precisely, as Rita Hamilton explains, Juan Ruiz treats matters in this section of the *Libro* which were topics of great clerical concern and controversy during his day. [5] The second attitude towards the discussion of confession sees it as serving a comical function. Zahareas, for example, articulates this view as follows: "The parodic digression of the misapplication of Christian rites strengthens the humor of this mock-epic narrative by adding the hilarious incongruity of the digression with the frame story [i.e., the battle between Cuaresma and Carnal]" (*The Art of Juan Ruiz*, p. 136).

After rehearsing the major critical appraisals, the textual evidence and the ecclesiastical disputes which were being waged at the time when Juan Ruiz was writing his book, Hamilton concludes that the content of the digression on confession "suggests that in this passage, more than in any other section of the *Libro,* the voice of the narrator may possibly be that of Juan Ruiz 'Arcipreste de Hita'" (Hamilton, p. 157). This is to say, that the author is interested in making known his own attitude towards the historically real controversy. Moreover, Hamilton sees this digression as being profoundly serious (unlike Zahareas): "There is no mistaking the scorn which Juan Ruiz shows for the friars by making one of them exercise the doubtful privilege of giving Don Carnal absolution" (Hamilton, p. 157).

Both perspectives are, in fact, admissible and plausible. For while it is very plausible to interpret the friar's role (and Don Carnal's also) as the object of the Archpriest's scorn, the "hilarious incongruity" which Zahareas notes may similarly be said to project

---

[5] Rita Hamilton, "The Digression on Confession in the *Libro de buen amor*," *'Libro de buen amor' Studies*, pp. 149-57.

the Archpriest's condemnation of those who trifle with the holy sacrament. Moreover, whereas the extra-textual information provided by Church history — while adding to the richness of this passage (which Lecoy [p. 198] and Hamilton [p. 157] deem inferior on thematic grounds) — it is not necessary for interpretation of the passage per se, or with respect to the Augustinian subtext either.

The key to interpretation lies in a distinction made in stanza 1138 which is further elaborated in stanza 1139:

> Quito es quanto a Dios, que es sabidor complido,
> mas quanto a la Iglesia, que non juzga de ascondido,
> es menester que faga, por gestos e gemido,
> sinos de penitencia que es arrepentido:
>
> en sus pechos feriendo, a Dios manos alçando,
> sospiros doloridos muy triste sospirando,
> sinos de penitencia de los ojos llorando;
> do más fazer non pueda, la cabeça enclinando.
>
> [One stands freed from sin in the eyes of God, who knows all; but for the Church, which does not judge hidden things, it is obligatory to make, by gestures and sighing, signs of penitence showing that one has repented:
>
> beating one's breast, raising one's hands to God, sadly sighing rueful sighs, shedding tearful signs of repentance from one's eyes; when one can do no more, nodding (one's) head.]

In these stanzas the Archpriest juxtaposes sincere contrition which absolves one from his sins in the eyes of the Lord, who knows all (sts. 1137c-d, 1138), and the Church, "que non juzga de ascondido" (st. 1138b) ["which does not judge hidden things"]. This seems a rather cynically conceived distinction, for it presents the Church as being caught up with outward displays of repentance. It is a real distinction, however, and is very aptly represented by Don Carnal, who confesses, sighs, and laments — but as we well know, he will very soon forget his confession of faith and his temporary contrition, acting sinfully for all but forty days out of 365 because he is never definitively converted. True confession involves renunciation (of fleshly concerns) and clearly Don Carnal is not capable of such renunciation. Instead he, as man in general, concerns himself with matters of the spirit primarily during the forty days of Lent, but even then, it is basically a concern for the outward manifestations of religiosity. It is no accident that Don Carnal's penance is defined in terms of dietary restrictions (as it is for all men during the Lenten season). Stanzas 1163-69 prescribe the various dishes which he should eat in order to demonstrate his spirit of repentance. No gesture of spirituality in the form of fasting or prayer is dictated to Don Carnal by his confessor, the friar. Hence both parties reveal themselves to be concerned merely with outward displays of contrition. This is, moreover, the human norm in general, as the Archpriest implies. The genuine spirit of confession as a profession of true faith is entirely ignored in this presentation of penance.

The presentation of penance does not stop here. Significantly, Juan Ruiz opposes such superficial transformations with examples of true conversion. Having established the distinction in stanza 1138 between God's knowledge of one's inner being (his spiritual existence) and absolution of the truly repentant sinner with the Church's demand for outward manifestation, the Archpriest offers us three examples of truly repentant Christians whose confession was a sign of their true, definitive conversion (none of whom, incidentally, relied upon confession by a clergyman):

> Que tal contrición sea penitencia bien llena,
> ay en la Santa Iglesia mucha prueva e buena.
> Por contrición e lágrimas la santa Madalena
> fue quita e assuelta de culpa e de pena.
>
> Nuestro señor Sant Pedro, tan santa criatura,
> negó a Jesucristo con miedo e con quexura;
> veo que lloró lágrimas tristes con amargura,
> otra satisfación non fallo en escritura.
>
> El rey don Ezequías, de muerte condenado,
> lloró, mucho contrito, a la pared tornado;
> de Dios tan piadoso luego fue perdonado:
> quinze años de vida eñadió al culpado. (sts. 1141-43)

> [That such contrition is truly full penance, there is in the holy Church abundant and excellent proof. By contrition and tears, the holy Mary Magdalene was freed and absolved of guilt and from punishment.
>
> Our master St. Peter, so saintly a person, denied Jesus Christ from fear and anguish; I read that he wept sorrowful tears bitterly; I find no (mention of) other satisfaction in Scripture.
>
> King Hezekiah, when condemned to die, wept most contritely with his face to the wall; he was straightaway pardoned by God, most merciful: He added fifteen years of life to the sinner.]

These three Biblical figures exemplify confession which leads to definitive conversion — unlike Don Carnal and humanity in general, which he exemplifies as does the Archpriest qua protagonist.

Finally, while presenting Don Carnal as an emblem of human confession which does not lead to definitive conversion, in contrast to Augustine, the digression on confession highlights yet another consistent concern witnessed in the Archpriest's text, namely his belief in the limits of exemplary discourse. The degree of exemplarity produced by a given didactic work is relative to the individual reader himself, as demonstrated above. A cleric may admonish the parishioner didactically and he in turn may, on a regular basis, profess his faith. Yet only those of good understanding are capable of incorporating the exemplary discourse communicated to them and of acting in an appropriately exemplary fashion thereafter. Those readers of poor understanding, "los simples" (st. 1634), will mechanically mouth the exemplary discourse of Christianity, yet they will not apply its substance, as Don Amor aptly illustrates. Thus the digression on confession serves as one more indication of Juan Ruiz's reading-theory, which itself is a logical extension of the Augustinian paradox.

VI. MISAPPROPRIATED *EXEMPLA*

Augustine dwells at length in the *Confessions* on the power of the moral *exemplum* as a persuasive rhetorical device. He explains, as we have seen, that he had read Scripture for many years prior to his conversion to Christianity. However, he had been unmoved by the power of God's Word since his flawed moral state made him unreceptive to its truth.[1] Yet once his will and intellect have merged in the pursuit of Christian truth, Augustine the protagonist finally understands — albeit partially — the power of Christ as moral exemplar, and of Scripture as global Christian *exemplum*. As Colish remarks:

> For Augustine ... God creates the world and man through His Word, and He takes on humanity in the Word made flesh so that human words may take on Divinity, thereby bringing man and the world back to God. In His redemptive plan, God has already solved for man the problem of His own ineffability. Once joined to God in Christ, human nature is restored in mind and body, and man's faculty of speech is empowered to carry on the work of Incarnation in expressing the Word to the world. For Augustine, redeemed speech becomes a mirror through which men may know God in this life by faith. And Christian eloquence becomes, both literally and figuratively, a vessel of the Spirit, bearing the Word to mankind, incorporating men into the Covenant of Christ, and preparing them through its mediation for the face-to-face knowledge of God in the beatific vision (Colish, p. 35).

---

[1] Colish, *The Mirror of Language*, p. 35.

Henceforth no distance separates Augustine the Christian behaviorally from the message of the *exemplum* which he offers as interlocutor. Such is not the case with Juan Ruiz's characters.

Considerable attention has been devoted to the use of *exempla* in the *Libro*. It is common knowledge that most of the instructive tales found therein were not created by the Archpriest himself, but rather that they pertain to the vast corpus of traditional didactic literature in the form of popular wisdom, of the sort found in collections of *exempla* and in oral literature as well (Lecoy, pp. 113-71).

Of this traditional subject matter two key points have been articulated by Ian Michael in terms of the *Libro*. First, that the thirty-five fables are encountered at moments of debate between two characters (e.g., the protagonist vs. Don Amor, Trotaconventos vs. Doña Endrina and Doña Garoça vs. Trotaconventos).[2] Second, that numerous fables as used in the *Libro* do not illustrate what they do traditionally, or even, what the given character is attempting to prove. That is to say, Juan Ruiz often does not attempt the most suitable illustration of the point being disputed: "After making one [often loose] connection between a tale and the outer framework, he felt free on occasion to exploit the tale for its own sake" ("Function," p. 216). Michael gives several very convincing examples of such misappropriated tales (numbers 12, 17, 21, 23 and 24, which correspond respectively to sts. 261-68, the tale of Virgil in the basket; sts. 321-71, the wolf who objects to the fox stealing the cockerel; sts. 529-43, the hermit who becomes a drunk, a rapist, and a murderer; sts. 766-79, the sow who kicks the wolf into a stream when he comes to baptize her young; and 892-906, the ass without a heart).

Both points elaborated by Michael are significant to the Archpriest's poetics in general and, in particular, they are consistent with the reading-theory discerned thus far in the *Libro*, and with his re-working of Augustine.

The tale of Pitas Payas (sts. 474-89) is a case in point. María Rosa Lida de Malkiel identifies this tale as a descendent of the *fabliau* tradition: "a true *fabliau* in its theme, structure, and

---

[2] Ian Michael, "The Function of the Popular Tale in the *Libro de buen amor*," '*Libro de buen amor*' *Studies*, p. 216.

licentious tone..." (*Two Spanish Masterpieces*, p. 8). Anthony Zahareas further analyzes this narrative in detail in terms of *fabliau* poetics:

> Juan Ruiz's appreciation of different ironic contrasts is clearly perceptible in the *dénouement* of the story. In the usual fabliau outcome, the husband discovers the infidelity and the unfaithful wife has to answer... Juan Ruiz, however, shifts the interest from the wife's infidelity to the husband's absence and to the ironic implications of their conversation. (*The Art of Juan Ruiz*, pp. 89-90)

Zahareas identifies two themes to be gleaned from this tale: "one having to do with a husband outsmarted by his young wife, the other with the problem of negligence in love which is part of the *ars amatoria*" (*The Art of Juan Ruiz*, p. 86).

Michael, on the other hand, sees only one possible moral to be gotten from this intercalated narrative, namely, the risks involved in neglectful love ("Function," p. 204). In his opinion, this shift in emphasis from the traditional didactic kernel to an amoral lesson is necessitated by the immediate narrative framework — in this case by Don Amor's enumeration of the commandments of his art of love.[3]

Yet what becomes clear from the conclusions reached both by Zahareas and Michael is that this tale (as so many others encountered throughout the *Libro*) is a polysemous text: it may be construed as an antifeminist reproach of feminine wiles and machinations delivered in a traditionally clerkly didactic tone or as a wholly untraditional amoral exemplification of the risks involved in being an unattentive lover. A third possible reading exists, as Michael points out from Stith Thompson's Motif Index, the traditional lesson imparted when this tale is invoked, namely, the real danger of becoming a cuckolded husband. Like the *Libro* as a whole then, this individual tale has several possible meanings. Its interpretation is contingent upon the particular understanding of the individual reader himself.

A number of other fables function in a similarly polysemous fashion. The twenty-first tale — that of the hermit who drinks to

---

[3] See also Donald Mc Grady, "The Story of the Painter and his Little Lamb," *Thesaurus*, 33 (1978), 357-406.

excess, becoming thereafter a rapist and murderer (sts. 529-43) illustrates yet again the built-in potential for multiple interpretations which the Archpriest as author wishes to underscore for his attentive reader. The standard moral which this tale imparts is that drunkenness leads to other more dangerous evils, e.g., loathsome and violent acts such as rape and murder. This is clearly the application projected by the fable as it occurs in the *Libro de Apolonio*.[4] Juan Ruiz, however, subordinates this lesson in order to foreground another. He devotes nearly three quatrains to an enumeration of the bad side-effects which an excess of wine produces on the lover: it gives him bad eyesight, shortens his life, reduces his stamina, gives him halitosis, etc. (sts. 544-46b). Only after completing this catalogue of detrimental physical effects which intoxication has on the lover does Don Amor mention (briefly) the didactic conclusion which is normally affixed to this fable:

> fazen muchas vilezas e todos los aborrecen;
> a Dios lo yerran mucho e al mundo fallecen. (st. 546c-d)
>
> [they do contemptible things and everyone despises them; they offend God greatly and lose standing with their fellowmen.]

Analyzing the primary didactic emphasis which Juan Ruiz places on this *exemplum* (that wine produces bad breath — thereby making the lover undesirable — not that it leads to much worse sins such as lust and murder), Michael observes that: "[Juan Ruiz] has adjusted the lesson to correspond to Don Amor's argument, but, just as his delight in story-telling in the tale of Virgil the enchanter leads to an imperfect adjustment, so here his urge to moralize temporarily blinds him to the situation in his main narrative and in 546-47 he extracts the full traditional moral from the tale. This produces a curious but momentary shift in Don Amor's position from that of an instructor in amatory skill to that of the medieval preacher ("Function," p. 205).

---

[4] Sts. 54-55.

The "urge to moralize," however, is exhibited by Don Amor, not by the narrator. Furthermore, the narrative shift which Michael correctly identifies here is in fact part of an extensive and consistent program of didactic inclinations exhibited by Don Amor, the protagonist, Trotaconventos, Doña Endrina and Doña Garoça. Likewise, Don Amor engages in an incongruous and rather lengthy fable in which, as in the tale of the hermit, he adopts the sermonic stance of a preacher, the "enxienplo de la propiedad qu'el dinero ha" (in stanzas 490-527). In his important essay Michael does not treat this subject matter since it does not, strictly speaking, function as a reworking of a traditional fable, but rather as a sermonic digression delivered from the pulpit. However, its implications for the use to which Juan Ruiz puts exemplary discourse (a clear extension of his reading-theory) are manifold. Don Amor prefaces his disquisition on the persuasive power of money in stanza 489 with the following uncourtly advice which he offers to the protagonist:

> Por poquilla cosa del tu aver que l'dieres,
> servirte ha lealmente, fará lo que quesieres;
> que poco o que mucho dal' cada que podieres;
> fará por los dineros todo quanto le pedieres.
>
> [For just a trifling amount of your money that you give her, she will serve you loyally, she will do as you want; whether it is a lot or a little, make a gift to her whenever you can; for money she will do all you ask of her.]

To dramatize his point, Money becomes personified by Don Amor in stanza 493, and is thereafter eulogized by the god of Love. "El dinero quiebra peñas e fiende dura madera" ("Money has the power to cleave stone and hard wood" [translation mine], st. 511d), as he tells us. This discourse on the mightiness of money could not be further in diction from the Ovidian commandments of love which Don Amor claims to represent. And, so that we do not miss the point of this radical departure from the dictates of courtly love, Don Amor shifts theme from the all-powerful effects of money in achieving amorous fulfillment to the benefits of beating the beloved:

> Quanto es más sossañada, quanto es más corrida,
> quanto es más por omne majada e ferida,
> tanto más por él anda loca, muerta, perdida;
> non cuida ver la ora que con él sea ida. (st. 520)
>
> A toda cosa brava grand uso la amansa.
> (st. 524a)

> [The more she is scolded, the more she is jeered at, the more she is beaten and struck by a man, the more she goes mad over him to the point of death and damnation; she is afraid she will never see the time when she can run off with him.
>
> Every wild animal can be tamed by constant company.]

These words could easily be the observations of a medieval preacher concerning the faults of women; their inconstancy, their disregard for authority and, therefore, their need to be strongly disciplined by their husbands. Both Don Amor's thoughts on the influence exerted by money over the female gender (and over society in general) as well as his remarks on the corrupt nature of women, can be construed didactically, in a morally exemplary manner. By the same token, however, they may be said to impart helpful advice on how to catch and keep a woman.

Thus once again, as in numerous other *exempla,* Juan Ruiz demonstrates on the one hand, the polysemous nature of his chosen text, that it will be glossed according to the particular understanding of a given reader. On the other hand, Don Amor's lengthy didactic disquisition proves once more that corrupt(ible), unexemplary characters are capable of producing exemplary discourse — without necessarily being converted themselves to a more exemplary mode of behavior. Such is the case with Don Carnal's confession without conversion — his cyclical, temporary repentance, during the Lenten season. Such is also the case with Doña Endrina and with Doña Garoça, both of whom show themselves to be veritable repositories of didactic wisdom which they display by the many exemplary fables which they deploy in their debates against Trotaconventos. (She too, of course, is full of the same kind of venerable Aesopic wisdom.)

Their ability to call to mind the litany of exemplary tales to which they have recourse in their dialogic exchanges repeatedly has no effect on their own wayward conduct.[5] A good illustration of this repeated pattern is afforded by the last bit of platitudinous wisdom offered by Doña Garoça (sts. 1454-84), the "Enxienplo del ladrón que fizo carta al diablo de su ánima" ["Fable of the robber who made a pact with the Devil for his soul"].

Michael writes informatively of this tale, identifying it as a traditional narrative found also in Berceo's *Milagro de Teófilo* and in Don Juan Manuel's *Libro del Conde Lucanor*:

> In this case the moral is firmly entrenched in the substance of the tale: those who sell their souls to the Devil will come to a bad end (though in Berceo's *Milagro de Teófilo*, which has a similar Faustian theme, there is, of course, a miraculous intervention by the Virgin). Perhaps because of the trenchancy of the moral, Juan Ruiz made this the last tale in the Doña Garoça episode; Trotaconventos's reaction to it is almost one of despair and she does not attempt to counter it with another tale: " 'Señora,' diz la vieja, 'muchas fablas sabedes.' " [" 'Lady,' said the old woman, 'you know a great many sayings' " (st. 1480a).] ("Function," p. 213)

As Michael notes, Trotaconventos does appear to give up trying to persuade Garoça at this point. Yet is it the trenchancy of Garoça's parable which causes the go-between to do so, or is it the fact that she knows that she has already won the battle? The four stanzas which follow Trotaconventos's ostensible acquiescence to the nun's argument cannot be ignored here, for they signal a complete reversal in Garoça's attitude:

> "Farías," dixo la dueña, "segund que ya te digo,
> lo que fizo el diablo al ladrón su amigo:
> dexarme ías con él sola e cerrarías el postigo;
> sería escarnida él fincando conmigo."
>
> Diz' la vieja: "Señora, ¡qué coraçón tan duro!
> D'esso que receledes ya yo vos asseguro,

---

[5] While Garoça's love for the Archpriest is chaste, she should not, in any event, be curious about him.

e de vos que non me parta en vuestras manos juro:
si de vos me partiere, a mí caya el perjuro."

La dueña dixo: "Vieja, non lo manda el fuero
que la mujer comience fablar amor primero;
cumple otear firme, que es cierto mensajero."
"Señora," diz', "el ave muda non faze agüero."

Dixo doña Garoça: "Que ayas buena ventura,
que d'esse acipreste me digas su figura,
bien atal qual sea, dime toda su fechura;
non respondas escarnio do te preguntan cordura."

(sts. 1481-84)

["You would do," said the lady, "as I have already told you, what the Devil did to his friend the thief: you would leave me alone with him and would lock the back door; I would be dreadfully deceived if he stayed with me."

Said the old woman: "Lady, what a hard heart! I give you my assurance against what you suspect, and swear on your two hands that I will not leave you: if I should leave you, may the guilt of perjury fall on me."

The lady said, "Old woman, it is not dictated by statute that the lady should be the first to begin the love talk; it is fitting to gaze very steadily, which is a sure way of conveying our message." "Lady," said the old woman, "a silent bird cannot utter omens."

Said Lady Bride: "May good fortune attend you, and please will you tell me what the Archpriest looks like; just as he is, tell me his entire appearance; don't give a mocking answer when someone asks you in earnest."]

Needless to say, this is a totally unexpected change of heart on the part of Garoça. Having just communicated the poignant example of the robber who sells his soul to the Devil, we are unprepared by the narrative to have her — literally in the next breath — capitulate to the go-between's invitation to meet the Archpriest. It is hard to imagine a more dramatic proof of the author's interest in illustrating the limits of exemplary discourse. (Nonetheless, the Archpriest affords us further evidence of this poetic procedure, for example, by having the protagonist's condemnation of Don Amor consist of an enumeration of the seven capital sins — while he is trying to learn from Don Amor how to attract women.) Like his readers, his interlocutors may avail themselves of much exemplary material without being affected by the didactic meaning which it bears.

One final aspect of the Archpriest's deployment of exemplary literature remains to be treated here. Namely, as Michael demonstrates with several different tales, Juan Ruiz does not in his chosen *exempla* offer close parallels to prove the point which is being debated at a given moment:

> There is always one bridge between the tale and the outer narrative, in a few cases there are two or more, but it is rare for the events or situation in the tale to match exactly those in the outer narrative ... it is possible that the faulty adjustments noted by Corominas [6] were not considered as such by Juan Ruiz: he may not have been aiming at fuller integration and thus, after making one connection between a tale and the outer framework, he felt free to exploit the tale for its own sake. ("Function," p. 216)

Michael's observation that Juan Ruiz was purposefully not trying to "fully integrate" the *exempla* into the narrative thread into which they are inscribed is quite convincing. Clearly, the at times distant relationship of the tale to the point it is ostensibly illustrating is a conscious decision by the author. It appears, moreover, that the Archpriest is not reproducing these traditional *exempla* simply "for their own sake." Rather these misappropriated fables are the product of a devious author figure calculated to create a distance between the didacticism of the tale itself and the enunciator of the tale — so as to make the attentive reader question the discernment of the enunciating subject, to underscore (like the rift separating what they practice from what they preach), their own unexemplary status.

---

[6] Joan Corominas, ed., *Libro de buen amor* (Madrid: Gredos, 1967), p. 53: "en cuanto a las Fábulas, los Cuentos ejemplares y algún trozo semejante, se tomó muy en serio la tarea de integrarlos dentro de su gran obra. Y, sin embargo, se advierten bien claras las suturas que las unen a esos conjuntos mayores..."

Viewed as an illustration (and thematization) of the limits of imitative literature, the *Libro* represents a real innovation in medieval narrative. And this is what the Archpriest implies when he claims in his prologue to be offering us a "new book." [7] As such, the *Libro* creates a radically new type of exemplary discourse.

---

[7] Significantly, he refers to his text as a "nuevo libro" (9) immediately before he discourses on the numerous ways in which it will be read (11, 13).

VII. THE CIRCULARITY OF STABLE IRONY

"Negation begins all ironic play," as Wayne Booth demonstrates in his study on the problematics of irony, *A Rhetoric of Irony*.[1] Irony calls upon the reader to reconstruct unspoken meanings after having rejected literal ones.

To say that the *Libro* is fraught with irony is an affirmation which few, if any, readers would dispute. Literal meaning must very often be rejected and an alternative sought. The reasons why the reader cannot accept literally what the Archpriest narrates in his book are various and complicated. There is first of all, the extensive short-circuiting of Auerbachian mimesis at issue in much of the *Libro*: the lengthy dream-vision in which the god of Love visits the Archpriest (sts. 181-575) in order to instruct him in the ways of love; the allegory of the two personification characters Lady Lent and Lord Meatseason (sts. 1067-1314), the adventures of the anthropomorphic mice (sts. 1370-86), etc. Also of paramount importance in alerting the reader to his important interpretive role is the fact that — as Zahareas meaningfully observes — the didactic distance separating the narrator from the protagonist is only apparent. "If Juan Ruiz were completely serious about the narrator's moral comments, he would surely have allowed that the commentator function more regularly, instead of only at intervals, and to function with more consistency" (*The Art of Juan Ruiz*, p. 30). What Zahareas does not do is to distinguish between narrator and author figure (or "implied author" in Booth's terminology), and this distinction is, as discussed above, of crucial significance.

---

[1] Wayne C. Booth, *A Rhetoric of Irony* (Chicago: Chicago University Press, 1974), p. 240.

Perhaps Zahareas' greatest contribution to *Libro* scholarship is his extensive analysis of irony in the Archpriest's poem — not simply with regard to the unreliability of the narrator on didactic terms, but rhetorically, thematically, narratively, etc. Yet by not distinguishing between the narrator and author figure, Zahareas is led to conclude that the *Libro* is the product of "unstable irony," as a text which generates so many ambiguities that the only clear meaning which remains constant throughout the text is the Archpriest's achievement qua poet (*The Art of Juan Ruiz*, p. 220). By not perceiving the importance of the implied author and the implied reader, Zahareas interprets the work as (necessarily) "unstable," which amounts to a dangerously anachronistic reading. Booth defines this form of irony by the following description: "What we do with a work, or what it does with us, will depend on our decision, conscious or unconscious, about whether we are asked by it to push through its confusion to some final point of clarity or to see through it to a possibly infinite series of confusions" (*Rhetoric*, p. 214). In what he perceives to be an "endless series of confusions" generated by Juan Ruiz, Zahareas sees his pride in his poetic craft as the only unironic value which the reader consistently discerns and which is never undercut. However, as Zahareas himself acknowledges, this kind of "art for art's sake" interpretation of an overtly Christian framework is quite incongruous in the light of fourteenth-century Spanish literature. Aware of this incongruity, he speaks of the Archpriest as a truly unique poet for his time: "This artistic awareness, combined with the temperament of *alegría*, leads Juan Ruiz to exploit ironic techniques so diverse that he stands apart from all other satiric or moral writers of the Spanish Middle Ages" (*The Art of Juan Ruiz*, p. 220).

Indeed, the Archpriest's techniques of irony are awesomely diverse and rich, yet they are not intended to produce the "endless series of confusions" which is the mark of unstable irony, but rather the circular series of constant but finite figurative meanings which define the scope of "stable irony." Speaking of this ironic form of discourse, Booth explains that: "when we apply it we imply a community of minds, and we depend, in the testing, on the validity of the process that is itself proved to be valid. It takes at least two to play this game in which the rules are reflexively established" (*Rhetoric*, p. 14). The community implied in the *Libro* is, clearly, the Christian populace of fourteenth-century Spain. (Within this community, of course, is implied a great disparity of understandings, given the Augustinian paradox of reading and readership which Juan Ruiz exploits.)

If we trace the "four steps of reconstruction" outlined by Booth, we will see that the *Libro* pertains to the mode of stable irony which closely accords with the Archpriest's theory of reading — indeed, forming the basis of this theory. The first step involves the reader's rejection of the literal meaning communicated by the text. We would all agree that Juan Ruiz qua protagonist did not literally meet the god of Love, that the assorted fish and vegetables which constitute Lady Lent's army are as fictitious as she is, that the book itself does not literally address its readers in a human voice, etc. Extratextual evidence is not required for us seriously to question literal mimesis (representation of things as they really are) as what is being presented in the *Libro*. Beyond such necessary denial of verisimilitude, the chief level of irony is generated by the cyclical structures discussed at length above in terms of textual detail. The protagonist and the narrator both claim to uphold one form of conduct, yet their behavior itself proves that they are otherwise — very often the opposite of what they claim. Similarly, the narrator's mutually contradictory definitions create ironic incongruity. His naming of the Christian love of God, the love of women, Trotaconventos and the book itself all as "buen amor" also forces the discerning reader to reflect on the work, in an attempt to reconstruct another more coherent explanation for these multiple associations than their wholly confusing literal equivalence. [2] This pursuit of alternative meanings leads to their tentative implementation. This is step two: "Alternative interpretations or explanations are tried out ... the alternatives will all in some degree be incongruous with what the literal statements seem to say — perhaps even contradictory, as one tra-

---

[2] See in this connection Charles V. Aubrun, "'Buen Amor': Approximations," *Homenaje a don Agapito Rey* ed., Joseph Roca-Pons (Bloomington: Department of Spanish and Portuguese, University of Indiana, 1980), pp. 73-89, and Brian Dutton, "*Buen amor*: Its Meaning and Uses in Some Medieval Texts," '*Libro de buen amor*' *Studies*, pp. 95-121.

ditional definition puts it, but certainly in some sense a retraction, diminution or undercutting: it is a slip, or he is crazy or I missed something earlier, or that word must mean something I don't know" (*Rhetoric,* p. 11). We have seen that in the case of the fables, the allegories of Love and Lent and indeed in just about every other form of narrative (except, significantly, the mariological and christological — which are strategically placed at the beginning, middle and end of the text),[3] numerous interpretations are possible, are in fact built into the Archpriest's presentation.

The third step in the process of reconstructing meaning involves a decision. Since one (or a group) of alternative meanings is more plausible than the literal one, we can only accept the more plausible. From this more plausible alternative (or set of alternatives) we are led to reflect upon the author himself — his knowledge or beliefs — in order to verify what we perceive as being the interpretation of the work as a whole on the basis of the plausible nonliteral meaning(s) which we have chosen. Clearly, "it is this decision about the author's own beliefs that entwines the interpretation of stable ironies so inescapable in intentions" (*Rhetoric,* p. 11). The decision concerning the author's basic values — which he projects entirely in his text — allows, finally, for a new interpretation of the text. The difference between the initial literal meaning which we perceive upon our first reading, and this latter reconstructed meaning or series of meanings has to do entirely with the reader. In speaking of Voltaire with respect to these two types of reading, Booth remarks that: "unlike the original proposition, the reconstructed meanings will necessarily be in harmony with the unspoken beliefs that the reader has decided [on the basis of textual evidence] to attribute to Voltaire" (*Rhetoric,* p. 12).

This is, of course, the case with Juan Ruiz as well, and he is acutely aware of this fact. By the consistent parody of earthly love he offers a preferred meaning — that of the Christian exegete — for those readers of discernment. Yet aware that he cannot persuade his readers to adopt this interpretation by dictating interpretation explicitly, he knows that those readers who are devotees

---

[3] Sts. 1-10, 11-19 are invocations to the Lord; sts. 20-32, 33-43 are *gozos* to the Virgin; sts. 1046-58, 1059-66 are poems commemorating the Passion of Christ; sts. 1635-41, 1642-49 are, once again, *gozos* in honor of the Virgin.

of *loco amor* will probably remain so. In the last analysis he is, as we have seen from the opening words of the prologue to the very last sentence of his book, profoundly aware of the limits of exemplary discourse. As author figure, however, he structures his text so that the implied (Christian) reader cannot fail to perceive the narrator-protagonist configuration as an *exemplum ex negativo*.

Returning to another important distinction made in Zahareas' study, we find that he juxtaposes irony and allegory in a section of his book entitled "The Subtlety of Medieval Texts: Allegory vs. Irony" (pp. 46-53). Again as before, Zahareas raises fundamental issues of the *Libro,* yet as with his conception of irony, his discussion of allegory is rather limited. This view stems from a desire to substantiate his thesis that the Archpriest's poem has "more artistic than ideological unity" (*The Art of Juan Ruiz,* p. 52). He minimizes the lasting importance of the Archpriest's remarks to the reader about the manner in which his text asks to be glossed: "The idea that it is the reader who chooses what he wants from a book is, of course, a well-known commonplace found in Capellanus, Boccaccio, and Chaucer. Many medieval writers warn the reader to take the good and abandon the bad. Only Juan Ruiz does not say what is good or bad, or if he does, he reciprocates the values good and bad" (*The Art of Juan Ruiz,* p. 52).

This is in fact an accurate portrayal of what the Archpriest literally tells us. But as he dramatizes throughout his book, the act of prescribing meaning for one's readers is ineffectual, returning once again to the premise of the Augustinian paradox. Furthermore, the author figure who refuses repeatedly to dictate what the good may be (content rather to imply it — as well as the bad), must be differentiated from the narrator and protagonist who occupy the time of writing and the time of the narrative. The narrative vacillation — the "reciprocation of the values good and bad" which Zahareas analyzes extensively belongs to the narrator and protagonist personae, not to the author figure and the "time of reading."

Much discussion has been devoted to the topic of allegory and the question of whether Juan Ruiz avails himself of this mode of writing. Foremost in this controversy is Thomas Hart's book, *La alegoría en el 'Libro de buen amor'*. This work offers a Robertsonian analysis of the text, which fails to deal with several key aspects of the Archpriest's composition. María Rosa Lida de Malkiel objects to Hart's view of the *Libro* as "Christian allegory" primarily because medieval allegorizers "glosan sistemáticamente todos o casi todos los términos del texto alegorizado" ("Hart," p. 342), whereas Juan Ruiz clearly does not. Moreover, Lida is concerned with underscoring what, in her view, is the primordial importance of the Hispano-Arabic *maqamat* for the *Libro*:

> La prescindencia del 'mudejarismo' cultural en que el *Libro* surgió ... ha privado al autor de un medio valioso para verificar su hipótesis, ya que en dicho contexto cultural el didacticismo intelectual y moral es tan obligado como inadmisible la alegoría mística a la manera de Rabano Mauro y Hugo de San Víctor. ("Hart," p. 344)

The other principal objection to Hart's reading originates from the fact that a Christian allegorical interpretation does not account for the considerable degree of "laughter" — humor — which the work undeniably contains. Alexander Parker, in reviewing Hart's study, emphasizes the essentially light-hearted tone of the *Libro*: "Above the *amor loco* of this world there is a joy and a hope that make it imperative for men, if they are to remain sane, to laugh about their own weakness. That his own sign language should be allegorized into solemnity is perhaps a joke that the Archpriest is enjoying in heaven." [4]

In this regard Zahareas distinguishes between allegory and irony, this latter mode being the one which he sees as the dominant one in the *Libro*: "Since allegory is utilized for a systematic interpretation, designed to produce in the reader the clear and certain understanding of a 'truth,' the indications concerning the other meaning are usually clear and precise. But if the central element in allegory is clarity, that of irony is paradox or ambiguity" (*The Art of Juan Ruiz*, p. 42). Booth explains that allegory and irony are not by any means necessarily opposing factors: "There is such a thing as ironic allegory, of course, and its effects are often the

---

[4] Alexander A. Parker, "Thomas R. Hart, *La alegoría en el 'Libro de buen amor'*. Madrid: Revista de Occidente, 1959 (*MLN*, 77 [1962], 559).

effects of stable irony. The explicit attack on communist (and other) totalitarianisms that we reconstruct in reading Orwell's *Animal Farm* is recreated against the grain of the literal evaluations offered by the surface of the tale" (*Rhetoric*, p. 25).

Analyzing the effect produced on the reader by allegory and irony, Booth further elaborates his point as follows:

> This distinction [between the two modes of discourse] is not merely of theoretical importance. For the reader there will always be a great difference between the traps laid by stable irony and the invitations offered by allegory. A naive reader who overlooks irony will totally misunderstand what is going on. A naive reader who reads an allegory without taking conscious thought, refusing all invitations to reconstruct general meaning out of the literal surface, will in effect obtain an experience something like what the allegory intends: the emotional and intellectual pattern will be in the direction of what it would be for the most sophisticated reader. (*Rhetoric*, p. 25)

Thus, while a literal-minded misreader of allegory will at least grasp the literal level of the text, a misreader of irony is quite another matter: "when someone is corrected about misreading an irony, he is shocked; he is being asked to repudiate all of his original response and move in an entirely new direction" (*Rhetoric*, p. 25).

The *Libro*, both in the meaning which it projects and in the interpretive act which it calls upon its reader to perform, reveals itself to be a form of allegory — namely, ironic allegory. At various points in the text we are reminded that, in addition to the literal interpretation which is generated, various figurative interpretations are possible, indeed are built into the text. As the parable of the Greeks and Romans narrates, and as Alexander Parker glosses it, the lesson to be understood is that: "All language is ambiguous in this sense: the serious reader will see that Juan Ruiz's book has a serious and didactic intention; the ribald reader, on the other hand, is bound to read it ribaldly. Similarly, the allegorizer, like his predecessors, the medieval exegetes, will not fail to find in it what he is looking for" (Parker, p. 559).

This is an extraordinarily significant statement, which Parker curiously treats as an off-hand remark rather than as a radically new authorial stance and as an essential heuristic tool for understanding the Archpriest's problematic text. For a medieval writer to acknowledge the ambiguity inherent in all language — or more precisely, the limits of exemplary discourse — is a profound innovation in poetic discourse. Indeed, this attitude which is the author's starting point in the composition of the text shows the *Libro* to be in its profoundest sense nothing less than an allegorization of the reading process. As such — as a thematization of possible multiple interpretations — it harkens back to the *Confessions* once more. The essential difference between the two texts is that the *Confessions,* as we have seen, functions as a Christian allegory of reading (the linguistic signs becoming positivistically unambiguous), whereas the *Libro* from beginning to end refers to a substantially wider range of possible readings (both Christian and non-Christian). The Christian interpretation is preferred — as witnessed by the deflationary treatment of earthly love throughout the work, and of man's feeble memory, his disinclination to act in accordance with the at times eloquent exemplary advice which he is capable of producing.

Finally, the various allegories of reading contained within the *Libro*: the ribald, the amatory, the Christian registers, etc., serve as a metaphor for man's reading of "God's Book" in two senses. First, one's comprehension of Scripture, which is read to him regularly in church, and in addition, of the world itself as God's book.

"Speculum mundi" and "Speculum lectoris"

In his encyclopedic documentation of medieval topological erudition, Curtius traces the roots of the various book metaphors which gained currency during the Middle Ages and continued to be exploited throughout the Renaissance:

> It is a favorite cliché of the popular view of history that the Renaissance shook off the dust of yellowed parchments and began instead to read in the book of nature or of the world. But this metaphor itself derives from the Latin Middle Ages. We saw that Alan speaks of the 'book of experience.' For him every creature is a book (PL CCX, 579A):

> Omnis mundo creatura
> Quasi liber et pictura
> Nobis est et speculum. (Curtius, p. 319)

Curtius further expatiates upon this metaphorical equivalence by producing examples from the Old and New Testaments (Curtius, pp. 310-11) and then refers to Prudentius (c. 400) as being the first example of this topos in the early Latin Middle Ages.

Noting that the twelfth-century renaissance brought with it a proliferation of book metaphors, Curtius details this phenomenon as articulated by Bonaventure, who speaks both of the world as a book and as God's book of creation: "creatura mundi est quasi quidam liber in quo relucet... Trinitas fabricatrix" (*Breviloquium* II, c. 12). In addition to the book of the world, however, Bonaventure stresses the importance of the *liber scripturae,* of which it is a reflection: "It is God's will that he be known through both books" (II, c. 5, Curtius, p. 321).

Surprisingly, however, Curtius fails to document the import of the *speculum mundi* in Augustine's literary system. For, the last four books of the *Confessions* are developed in terms of a conflation of these two book metaphors: the world as God's metaphorical book, just as Scripture is God's literal Book.

Book XIII of Augustine's text offers a revealing illustration of the intertwining of these two metaphors:

> Sunt aliae aquae super hoc firmamentum, credo, inmortales et a terrena corruptione secretae. laudent nomen tuum, laudent te supercaelestes populi angelorum tuorum, qui non opus habent suspicere firmamentum hoc et *legendo* cognoscere verbum tuum. vident enim faciem tuam semper, et ibi *legunt* sine syllabis temporum, quid velit aeterna voluntas tua. *legunt,* eligunt et diligunt; semper *legunt* et numquam praeterit quod *legunt.* eligendo enim et diligendo *legunt* ipsam incommutabilitatem consilii tui. *non clauditur codex eorum* nec plicatur liber eorum, quia tu ipse illis hoc es et es in aeternum. (404, 406)

> [Above this firmament of your Scripture (the physical sky which the human eye perceives, as well as the earth beneath it) I believe that there are other waters, immortal and kept safe from earthly corruption. They are the peoples of your city, your angels, on high above the firma-

ment. Let them glorify your name and sing your praises, for they have no need to look up to this firmament of ours or *read* its text to know your world. For ever they gaze upon your face and there, without the aid of syllables inscribed in time, they *read* what your eternal will decrees. They *read* your will: they choose it to be theirs: they cherish it. They *read* it without cease and what they *read* never passes away. For it is your own unchanging purpose that they *read,* choosing to make it their own and cherishing it for themselves. *The book they read shall not be closed.* For them the scroll shall not be furled. For you yourself are their book and you for ever are.] [5]

Such thematization of reading and the equivalence of this earth, of Scripture and of God Himself with the book is as highly significant for Augustine's system of reading as it is for Juan Ruiz's.

Reading is endowed with tremendous importance both literally — the reading of and reflection upon Scripture — and metaphorically as the assimilation and implementation of God's Word in man's daily existence on earth. It is, moreover, this image of God's unending creation as text ("the book which shall not be closed") which Juan Ruiz recalls metaphorically at the end of the *Libro* (st. 1626):

> Porque Santa María, segund que dicho he,
> es comienço e fin del bien, tal es mi fe,
> fiz'le quatro cantares, e con tanto faré
> punto a mi librete, mas non lo cerraré.

> [Because the Holy Virgin, as I have said, is the beginning and the end of all good, so I do believe, I composed four songs for her, and thereupon I shall put an end to my book, but I shall not close it.]

By recalling "the book which shall not be closed" the Archpriest exploits his Augustinian subtext in a way which is in keeping with his implicit presentation of the act of reading. For while Augustine

---

[5] Pp. 322-23 (Emphasis mine). See in this regard, Eugene Vance, "Augustine's *Confessions* and the Poetics of the Law," *MLN*, 98 (1978), 618-34, esp. 632-34.

is referring to those men who have attained salvation in the afterlife (whom we should seek to emulate), the narrator-protagonist of the *Libro* is as distracted by earthly temptation at the end of his narration as he was at the outset. Rather than glossing this Augustinian reminiscence in a doctrinal manner, therefore, the Archpriest shows how it may be misconstrued by the unwise reader:

> Buena propiedad ha: doquiera que se lea,
> que si lo oyere alguno que tenga muger fea,
> o si mujer lo oyere que su omne vil sea,
> fazer a Dios servicio en punto lo desea. (st. 1627)
>
> [It has a good trait: wherever it may be read, if some man hears it who has an ugly wife, or if a woman hears it whose husband is of no account, each will immediately feel the desire to serve God.]

Clearly, the reader of *buen entendimiento* will understand the scriptural resonance and its implications — as well as the joke which he generates as one of the multiplicity of interpretations which he inscribes within his text.

Discussing the appropriateness of the *speculum* for the title of the journal of the Medieval Academy of America, E. K. Rand saw it as being powerfully suggestive of the "multitudinous mirrors in which people of the Latin Middle Ages liked to gaze at themselves and other folk — mirrors of history and doctrine and morals, mirrors of princes and lovers and fools." [6]

In a historical survey of the metaphor of the mirror and its importance for the Middle Ages, Ritamary Bradley begins her essay by acknowledging the complexities of this topic: "The religious subject matter in many of the early treatises may lead us to assume the influence of I Corinthians xiii, 12 and of the Epistle of St. James, i, 23-24. [7] Yet there is at once a difficulty: the Pauline

---

[6] E. K. Rand, "Editor's Preface," *Speculum*, 1 (1926), p. 4.

[7] "Videmus nunc per speculum in aenigmate: tunc autem facie ad faciem" (I *Cor*, xiii, 12); "Quia si quis auditor est verbi, et non factor: hic comparabitur viro consideranti vultum nativitatis suae in speculo: consideravit enim se, et abiit, et statim oblitus est qualis fuerit" (*James*, i, 23-24). See Ritamary Bradley, "Backgrounds of the Title *Speculum* in Medieval Literature," *Speculum* 29 (1954), 100-115.

text refers to enigmatic mirrors, whereas the literary mirrors are clear; and the text in St. James concerning the man who beheld his face in a glass and at once forgot what manner of man he was does not immediately suggest the key idea of paragon, not to mention many other figurative implications" (Bradley, p. 102).

Bradley, citing from numerous Church fathers in the light of what she terms the *"speculum* genre" (Bradley, p. 108) establishes the origins of the mirror metaphor for sacred and secular texts. Moreover, she explains, the mirror was not always a simple reflection of virtue. Referring to Gregory the Great's gloss of Augustine's commentary on Psalm 103, Bradley demonstrates how the mirror may at times be an *exemplum ex negativo* — the very opposite of a model to be imitated:

> Holy Scripture relates the deeds of the saints and admonishes the hearts of the weak to imitate them. While it reminds us of their victorious deeds, their warfare against vices, it strengthens our weakness... But sometimes it informs us not only of their virtues but familiarizes us with their falls, so that we may see in the victory of the great what we have to fear. (Bradley, p. 109)

Hence the *speculum* may function either imitatively or representationally. Indeed, Augustine builds both the imitative and representational modes of discourse into the *Confessions*. In his work the representational leads to the imitative. Although Bradley makes no mention of the *Confessions* in her well documented study, Augustine presents both his autobiography and the world itself specularly, as mirror. Having just established a metaphorical association between God's everlasting creation — the "scroll which shall not be furled," Augustine speaks of the "scroll which *shall* be folded" — namely, the physical universe:

> scriptura vero tua usque in finem saeculi super populos extenditur. sed et caelum et terra transibunt, sermones autem tui non transibunt, quoniam et pellis plicabitur, et faenum, super quod extendebatur, cum claritate sua praeteriet, verbum autem tuum manet in aeternum; quod nunc *in aenigmate* nubium et *per speculum* caeli, non sicuti est... (406).

> [your Scripture is outstretched over the peoples of this world to the end of time. Though heaven and earth should pass away, your words will stand. The scroll shall be folded and the mortal things over which it was spread shall fade away, as grass withers with all its beauty; but your Word stands forever. Now we see your Word not as he is, but dimly, through the clouds, *like a confused reflection in the mirror* of the firmament...][8]

Thus while offering us a model of Christian salvation, Augustine at the same time acknowledges our inability to see clearly in the mirror because of our human limitations. It is, as we have seen, primarily the representational (rather than the imitative) function of this mirror which Juan Ruiz chooses to exemplify in his poetry as a consequence of his belief in the limits of exemplary discourse. Those readers who are of good understanding will perceive the exemplary Christian quality inherent in this mimetic human mirror — which constitutes a distortion, a series of imperfect reflections (hence refractions) of the divine mirror. As such, i.e., by allowing for the interpretations of good and wayward readers simultaneously, Juan Ruiz's *speculum lectoris* represents a new permutation within the *speculum* canon.

---

[8] Bk. XIII, xv, p. 323 (Emphasis mine).

VIII. GENRE AS MEANING

"All understanding of verbal meaning is necessarily genre-bound," as E. D. Hirsch reminds us in his analysis of genre as hermeneutic concept.[1] Hence, if the Augustinian text is to be acknowledged as the principal subtext and conceptual wedge for understanding the *Libro,* it must also serve to elucidate Juan Ruiz's concept of literary genre.

Recognizing the need to identify a model text which can help to explain the *Libro*'s form as well as its semantic content, scholars have looked to numerous genres in their pursuit of meaning.

Two fundamental ascriptions of generic filiation have emerged over the decades of *Libro* criticism. The first (represented by Menéndez Pidal, Lecoy, Spitzer, and Zahareas) views the text essentially as an anthology or miscellany. The second critical attitude (represented by Castro, Lida de Malkiel, Rico, Nepaulsingh, and Michalski) emphasizes its primary generic identity as being some form of autobiographical narrative. This latter group which finds autobiography to be the basic generic model is further subdivided into Christian, Hebraic, Arabic and Ovidian forms. Finally, Gybbon-Monypenny combines aspects of both genres, finding the *Libro* to be a member of the generic hybrid which he entitles the "erotic pseudo-autobiography," a tradition which is firmly rooted in the conventions of courtly love ("Autobiography," pp. 63-78).

Menéndez Pidal sees the Archpriest's work as a non-didactic product of a *juglar:* it is not "un libro didáctico en serio; es un brote muy tardío... la despedida humorística a la época didáctica

---

[1] E. D. Hirsch, *Validity in Interpretation* (Chicago: Chicago University Press, 1967), p. 76.

de la literatura medieval" (*Poesía juglaresca,* p. 209). Félix Lecoy carefully details the Latin traditions which Juan Ruiz exploits in the forging of his text — the two major episodes of Doña Endrina and Lady Lent's battle against Lord Meatseason, and all the minor ones. From this breathtaking display of generic virtuosity, however, Lecoy confesses that it is difficult to discern a coherent theme in the work. It is an art of love but also has a moral dimension. Of this thematic incompatibility Lecoy concludes: "Juan Ruiz, ne l'oublions pas, n'est ni un philosophe ni même un moraliste — c'est un poète et comme tel, il a suivi son inspiration là où elle le guidait: si cette inspiration était parfois contradictoire, si elle connaissait des retours étonnants, des variations qui semblent étranges, avons-nous pour cela le droit de lui demander des comptes?" (Lecoy, p. 364).

While the *Libro*'s humor leads Menéndez Pidal to view it as an essentially humorous work, Leo Spitzer arrives at a substantially different conclusion: "El *Libro de buen amor* cuenta locuras, porque la necia conducta de los hombres es también el orden querido por Dios" ("En torno al arte," p. 134). Zahareas examines both the *Libro*'s anthological form and its autobiographical framework (although he minimizes the importance of this framework), and concludes from it that "All we can assume in explaining the Archpriest's comments, is that the *Libro* itself is a miscellany disposed chiefly towards secular notions, that these notions are incorporated into the conventional device of autobiographical frame, and that this frame is intended both to teach something serious and to entertain" (*The Art of Juan Ruiz,* p. 52). The unity of the *Libro* in Zahareas's estimation, resides in the Archpriest's display of his poetic craft.

Of those critics who endow the autobiographical frame with the greatest generic importance insofar as the production of meaning is concerned, Américo Castro adopts the Arabic model of the *risala*, rather than any Christian example. Concentrating on the *Libro*'s "forma fluida y deslizante" ("El *Libro de buen amor,*" p. 199), Castro finds it to be a reflection of daily medieval Spanish life: "Juan Ruiz interpretó temas de la tradición cristiano-europea con sensibilidad hispano-musulmana" ("El *Libro de buen amor,*" p. 202). Thus he views the *Libro* as proof of his historical thesis regarding the close proximity of the Arabic and Spanish cultures.

In *The Structure of Spanish History* Castro elaborates this view, affirming that "When Christians spoke in the first person on matters of morality, they did not at the same time express pleasure in the sensual charms of this world." [2] Countering this judgment as a clear sign that the *Libro* is rooted in Arabic rather than Christian narrative, Nepaulsingh brings up the example of Augustine: "When St. Augustine confesses, he frequently admits that his sins were beautiful and charming even though later, as a convert, he perceived not only their beauty but their underlying distress" ("Structure," p. 60). While Augustine in his pre-converted condition was very much influenced by sensual pleasures ("ego adulescens... petieram a te castitatem et dixeram: 'da mihi castitatem et continentiam, sed noli modo' " [Bk. VIII, vii 440]) ["As a youth... I had prayed to you for chastity and said 'Give me chastity and continence, but not yet'," (169)], it is inaccurate to say that as a convert he perceived the beauty of his sins. A definitive change in perspective occurs at the time of his conversion. While Nepaulsingh is correct in looking to Augustine as an epistemological device by which to explicate Juan Ruiz's text, his interpretation is hindered because he does not perceive the all-important distinction between narrator and author figure. [3]

María Rosa Lida de Malkiel's attribution of the Archpriest's poem to the tradition of the Hispano Hebraic *maqamat* (rather than the Hispano Arabic *risala* which Castro posits) stems from her disagreement with Castro as to the *Libro*'s most basic defining characteristic. She sees its didacticism as being more important than the oscillating structure upon which Castro bases his claim.

Francisco Rico's attribution of the *De Vetula* as the model text similarly falls short of explaining all of the major dimensions of the Spanish text. He provides a wealth of valuable information concerning the reception of Ovid in fourteenth-century Europe and, moreover, he underscores what he rightly judges to be the decidedly Western orientation of the *Libro* as autobiography: "Estos y semejantes usos del 'yo' en la literatura medieval eran

---

[2] Américo Castro, *The Structure of Spanish History*, trans. Edmund L. King (Princeton: Princeton University Press, 1954), pp. 102-03.

[3] Cf. pp. 59-73 above.

otros tantos refuerzos al planteo autobiográfico del *Libro de buen amor:* planteo, a mi entender, ajeno a todo influjo literario no occidental y perfectamente comprensible en la tradición ovidiana, en especial a la luz del 'De Vetula.' " [4] Rico goes far in making suggestive intertextual comparisons between the two texts. Yet the Ovidian tradition is clearly insufficient in accounting for the text as a whole, for the Ovidian material constitutes only a portion of the entire text in terms of subject matter.

Nepaulsingh's interpretation of the *Libro* as a hagiographic parody and Michalski's independently arrived-at interpretation of it specifically as a parodic inversion of the *Confessions* similarly afford only partial views of the *Libro,* whose form R. S. Willis has very justifiably termed "protean" ("Two Trotaconventos," p. 362). The conclusions of Nepaulsingh and Michalski are, first of all, based on a linear structure (culminating with the triumph of Don Amor) which, as we have seen, does not constitute a definitive triumph. Moreover, the autobiographical form which they posit does not justify the strongly anthological quality of the book.

Finally, Gybbon-Monypenny offers another explanation of the *Libro* as a parodic treatment of courtly love: "The erotic pseudo-autobiography was a serious Courtly genre. The *Libro de buen amor* seems to hold up to it a distorting mirror, showing its essential features in caricature" ("Autobiography," p. 77). The text does indeed parody the linguistic and amatory registers of courtly love, however the text similarly treats much material which has little or nothing to do with courtly love, hence with its specular distortion.

Obviously either the *cancionero* and/or autobiographical arguments are insufficient indications of the work's protean nature. This is, I would suggest, also in keeping with the reading theory projected by the Archpriest in his re-writing of Augustine.

While dramatizing the limits of exemplary discourse, as detailed at length with respect to the Augustinian paradox, Juan Ruiz asserts above all, human plurality, consequently, human diversity. Different people (readers) embody a multiplicity of perspectives — of moral states — as Augustine explains. Juan Ruiz is interested in mime-

---

[4] Francisco Rico, "Sobre el origen de la autobiografía en el *Libro de buen amor,*" *Anuario de Estudios Medievales,* 4 (1967), 325.

tically representing this human diversity rather than in offering an explicit model which he attempts to impose on his readers, a model to be overtly imitated. He exploits genre in order to underscore human complexity — precisely as he exploited theme — unconvinced that exemplary discourse will persuade those readers who are not of good understanding to become so.

A given genre is, in its broadest sense, a system of particular conventions. Moreover, this system of conventions produces a particular system of "generic expectation" [5] in the reader. Within any one genre we find projected "representative" actions of a representative human type. Hence the lyric persona is contemplative, the epic is heroic, the dramatic is theatrical, and so on. Man becomes of necessity reduced to a type as soon as he is cast in terms of a given generic mould. But just as Juan Ruiz exploits structure and theme in order to show human complexity (man's protean, problematic nature), so too he — logically, and innovatively — exploits genre. Not content to present man as a circumscribed type, he intentionally offers us instead a whole spectrum of types by exploiting a whole storehouse of generic traditions or frames of reference.

We see glimpses of man as devout Christian in the *Gozos de Santa María* which open and close the text as we do with the poems on the theme of Christ's Passion following the *serrana* episodes; we see him profaning Christian love with Cruz and the canonical hours, we see him apotheosize earthly love just as we see him also berate it. In short, as Zahareas astutely observes, "almost everything in the *Libro* is mentioned at least twice: once in earnest and once in jest" (*The Art of Juan Ruiz,* p. 140).

The necessary corollary to offering a compendium of generic modes in succession, held together by a slender narrative thread, is that our generic expectations are repeatedly, in fact continually, being undercut, "short-circuited," as it were. In an important study on genre (focusing specifically on the use of generic terminol-

---

[5] "toute œuvre littéraire appartient à un genre, ce qui revient à affirmer purement et simplement que toute œuvre suppose l'horizon d'une attente, c'est-à-dire d'un ensemble de règles préexistant pour orienter la compréhension du lecteur (du public) et lui permettre une réception appréciative" (Jauss, "Littérature médiévale et théorie des genres," p. 82).

ogy), Alan Deyermond points out that the *Libro* "contains nearly one hundred and thirty [generic] terms, used on nearly three hundred and fifty occasions." [6] As this study attests, the Archpriest clearly wished to project his text as, among other things, a generic compendium.

The effect of this presentation is predictable given Juan Ruiz's theory of reading, hence of human nature. No sooner have we as readers established that the protagonist represents the Ovidian lovestruck youth or the repentant sinner, the mock-epic narrator, the bawdy cleric, or any other in a veritable gallery of protagonist personae than he is immediately cast into another. Indeed it is not simply the protagonist who undergoes such protean characterological transformations, but Trotaconventos as well. [7] Other major characters such as Doña Endrina, Doña Garoça and Don Amor similarly undergo transformations in accord with the two different stances they adopt alternatively: that of an exemplary voice of Christian wisdom and morality or of purely earthly concerns.

Finally, this unprecedented generic compendium and exploitation is directly related to Augustine's reiterated attitude towards poetic fiction as expressed in the *Confessions*.

In Book III Augustine describes himself as having been a poet in his youth:

> et cantabam carmina, et non mihi licebat ponere pedem quemlibet ubilibet, sed in alio atque alio metro aliter et in uno aliquo versu non omnibus locis eundem pedem; (124, 126)

> [When I composed verses, I could not fit any foot in any position that I pleased. Each metre was differently scanned and I could not put the same foot in every position in the same line (64).]

He views this technical intricacy not as a welcome challenge to perfect his art, but rather as a sign of the inherent imperfection of poetic fiction per se:

---

[6] A. D. Deyermond, "Juan Ruiz's Attitude to Literature," *Medieval, Renaissance and Folklore Studies in Honor of John Esten Keller*, p. 115.

[7] See Willis, "Two Trotaconventos," pp. 353-62.

> et ars ipsa, qua canebam, non habebat aliud alibi, sed omnia simul. (126)

> [And yet the art of poetry, by which I composed, does not vary from one line to another: it is the same for all alike. (64)]

This paradoxical statement is calculated by Augustine as a way of communicating what for him is the inferiority of the discourse of "poetic truth" by comparison with religious truth:

> non intuebar iustitiam, cui servirent boni et sancti homines, longe excellentius atque sublimius habere simil omnia quae praecipit, et nulla ex parte varie, tamen variis temporibus non omnia simul, sed propria distribuentem ac praecipientem. (126)

> [I did not discern (at the time of the narrative) that justice, which those good and holy men obeyed, in a far more perfect and sublime way than poetry contains in itself at one and the same time all the principles which it prescribes, without discrepancy... (64)]

Similarly, in Book I, xiii Augustine speaks at length of the "emptiness" and "mock reality" of the pagan literature which he read as a schoolboy, specifically of the *Aeneid*. [8]

In his discussion of poetry, Augustine does not include devotional verse while Juan Ruiz clearly does. For Augustine, glossing a pre-existing sacred text (including the writing of prayers or of his confession) is the only activity within the purview of admissible activities for a Christian writer. It is obviously the creative dimension of poetic activity which Augustine condemns on two counts. Colish succinctly articulates this negative attitude towards poetic creation as follows: "The poets, he says, use words erroneously, since they use them to refer to things and ideas which are non-existent or untrue. Furthermore, he adds, the poets depict ignorant and irresponsible actions in their fictitious characters, who

---

[8] See pp. 38-42 for his discussion of Virgil. On p. 42 he writes similarly of the Greek texts which, along with the Virgilian text, he terms (from the perspective of the time of writing) "noxious pleasures" ("iucunditate pestifera," p. 44).

operate in accordance with the unreal universe of the author's creation. The beauty of this poetry is doubly dangerous, according to Augustine, since it is used to construct a world of shadows and to make the fantastic morality of that world attractive and convincing" (Colish, p. 25).

There is thus no room in Augustine's philosophy of poetic fiction for viewing such fiction as a potentially exemplary medium. For Juan Ruiz, on the other hand, there is. The key to whether the text's exemplary nature is perceived lies in the status of the reading subject. The Archpriest's clearly fictional text can be as potentially exemplary as Augustine's historically real text.

The *Libro* is, as numerous scholars have noted, and as Lecoy has admirably demonstrated, in an overt sense an encyclopedia of well established traditional (universal) subject matter, plots and generic constructs (Latin, vernacular, Christian, Hebraic and Arabic). By exploiting such traditional material the Archpriest, among other things, underscores the universal applicability of his text, allowing each reader to personally identify with the *Libro,* and to cull from it whatever lesson he may. In addition, the *Libro*'s self-conscious presentation as poetic *summa* underscores its fictionality. This fictional quality, moreover, accords perfectly with his theory of reading. For just as Juan Ruiz does not believe that reading can make converts of his readers — so too he disagrees with Augustine on the distinction which the latter formulates between the value of "true history" as represented by his own autobiography and by Scripture in general, as opposed to the total worthlessness, for Augustine, of poetic fiction. For Juan Ruiz, on the other hand, neither type of writing will have a necessarily exemplary effect on the reader — and *fabula* (fiction) is, therefore, as potentially instructive as *historia* (non-fiction).

Hence the Archpriest effects a kind of symmetrical transformation of his Augustinian model as a result of his consistent theory of reader-response: while not viewing imitative non-fiction as necessarily eliciting an exemplary response in his audience, similarly, fiction may be understood by a given audience exemplarily. These two attitudes are, in addition, logically necessary corollaries of one another. They underscore the creativity inherent in the act of reading, the reader's all-important interpretive role, while at the same time serving to valorize the status of poetic fiction itself.

The Augustinian subtext thus does much to explain the Archpriest's insistence on his own poetic prowess — a recurring motif of the *Libro* which has traditionally puzzled critics. For, by praising his rare abilities as poet, he signals to his audience that the text is intended to be appreciated in the light of its artistic merits, as being artistically exemplary and therefore worthy of admiration and praise. Yet he refuses to offer his readers any other guidelines by which the subject matter of his work should be appreciated or interpreted (thus ostensibly playing down its thematic dimension, thereby leading some interpreters to view it as to be taken seriously only on its artistic level, as *cancionero*). If the text is meant to function didactically, they reason, why would the author refrain from informing his readers of that fact, dwelling instead on his technical mastery of poetic forms? Surely if he had had a serious moral purpose it is logical to assume that he would communicate it even more explicitly and fully than his artistic purpose.

Given the Augustinian condemnation of poetry, I would suggest that the Archpriest's motives are not difficult to discern. Namely, he highlights his poetic abilities as a direct response to Augustine's challenge — to his absolute deflation of poetic discourse.

This avowedly problematic emphasis on art where we would expect an emphasis on didactic instruction shows Juan Ruiz not only responding to Augustine, but poetically "correcting" his predecessor's limited interpretation of the uses of fiction. Nonetheless, a careful reading of the final stanza of the narrative proper (st. 1634) in which the reader is directly addressed, offers a revealing indication concerning the degree of importance which we are asked to accord to the Archpriest's poetic mastery. It is in fact a startling indication, for in the two manuscripts (*S* and *T*) in which this stanza is extant, Juan Ruiz concludes his poem with the following admission:

MS T
> Era de mill e trezientos e sesenta e ocho años
> fue acabado este libro, por muchos males e daños
> que fazen muchos e muchas a otros con sus engaños,
> e por mostrar a los simples fablas e versos estraños.

[In the year of the Era of Caesar Augustus, one thousand, three hundred and sixty-eight (A.D. 1330), this book was finished, for many evils and wrongs that many men and women do to others with their deceits, and to display to simple people exemplary tales and ingenious verses.] [9]

From this statement of purpose we see that although the Archpriest repeatedly boasts of his poetic abilities, he ends his narrative by saying that his "ingenious verses" are intended for the "simple readers" — as are the *exempla* which are interspersed throughout it. Obviously, as the Archpriest was well aware, simpletons are incapable of appreciating ingenious verses or exemplary tales beyond their surface meaning.

This stanza has often posed a problem for modern readers, since its meaning seems obscure. Zahareas, while justifiably detailing the Archpriest's pride in his poetic accomplishments — the fact that he sees himself as rare indeed ("tú non fallarás uno de trobadores mil" [65d], "you won't find here just one of a thousand troubadours"), [10] does not address himself to the problematic admission of stanza 1634. For while Zahareas sees the *Libro* as having "more artistic than ideological solidarity," (*The Art of Juan Ruiz*, p. 52) the admission of stanza 1634 would appear to refute this claim. [11]

If the simple reader is the one for whom the ingenious poetry and exemplary tales are being displayed, then there exists also a

---

[9] *Ms* S

> Era de mill e trezientos e ochenta e un años
> fue conpuesto el romançe, por muchos males e daños
> que fazen muchos e muchas a otras con sus engaños,
> e por mostrar a los simples fablas e versos estraños.

[10] Zahareas (*The Art of Juan Ruiz*, p. 172) translates st. 65d as Juan Ruiz referring to himself as "one in a thousand poets," which overstates the Archpriest's actual words.

[11] In his study "El epílogo del *Libro de buen amor*," Nicolás Emilio Álvarez voices a different view concerning the "simples," identifying them as those people who are unfamiliar with the rules of poetry: " 'synplex' no hay que entenderse peyorativamente, sino como esos 'algunos' que desconocen la 'ciencia' poética y 'fablas e versos estraños' son los compuestos conforme a dicha ciencia los cuales podrán parecer extraños para los que no están familiarizados con las reglas poéticas" (p. 145).

more sophisticated reader whom Juan Ruiz implies. He is the reader who will go beyond the literal formal and thematic level, he is the one who is able, by his good understanding, to write metaphorically the gloss which the Archpriest calls for in stanzas 1631 and 1632a-b:

> Fiz'vos pequeño libro de testo, mas la glosa
> non creo que es chica, ante es bien grand prosa;
> ca sobre cada fabla se entiende otra cosa,
> sin lo que se alega en la razón fermosa.
>
> De la santidad mucha es muy grand licionario,
> mas de juego e de burla es chico breviario...
>
> [I have made you a book that is small in terms of text, but the exegesis, I believe, is not brief, rather it is a good big piece of writing; for in respect to each tale something else is to be understood, apart from what is said in the pretty wording.
>
> It is a very big doctrinal book about a great deal of holiness, but it is a small breviary of fun and jokes...]

The text remains necessarily polysemous, as does the very term *buen amor* (simultaneously denoting the *fin'amor* of courtly love and the Christian love of God). The task of interpretation thus remains each reader's problem — as Augustine himself acknowledged, but from a very different perspective.

Hence the *Libro* functions, among other things, as a dramatization of the Augustinian paradox. It is a mimetic, representational text which poetically "corrects" Augustine's imitative text — it is a confession without conversion. Moreover, it is largely in the Archpriest's re-orientation of Augustine that the *Libro*'s unity resides.

IX. CONCLUSION: JUAN RUIZ AND THE *MESTER DE CLERECÍA*

The semantic field of the term *clerecía* (clerkliness) — its definition — continues to attract substantial critical attention and controversy. The attempt to define the parameters of *clerecía* globally stems from a desire to discern some kind of coherent poetic system operative throughout the *mester de clerecía* corpus of the thirteenth and fourteenth centuries. This endeavor, moreover, has a direct bearing upon the *Libro,* which exploits the *clerecía* quatrain, the *cuaderna vía,* as its prevailing metrical form.

The term *mester de clerecía* designates a group of some of the most important and innovative literary works of medieval Spain: the learned, clerkly vernacular poetry. Yet the designation of this disparate group of masterpieces (indeed, the functional status of the rubric itself) has been consistently and deeply problematic for modern readers of medieval texts.

The conventional modern view recognizes the emergence of a new kind of poetic enterprise over the course of the thirteenth century: informed by *clerecía* ("clerkly learning"), articulated primarily in a single metricostanzaic form (the *cuaderna vía*) and exploiting the traditional narrative genres of the vernacular medieval canon (epic, hagiography, romance). The extraordinary prestige and vitality of this poetic phenomenon is generally assumed to have disappeared by the end of the thirteenth century. In fact, it is often assumed that serious interest in *clerecía* poetry simply could not be rekindled after Juan Ruiz's brilliant parody of it. The corpus of fourteenth-century clerkly poetry is thus, in effect, judged against the standard of the thirteenth and is found wanting.

As López Estrada has recently observed, the term *mester de clerecía* was artificially and anachronistically construed (for largely nationalistic and positivistic reasons) in the nineteenth century by Menéndez Pelayo as a self-consciously homogeneous and uniquely Spanish "poetic school." [1] In this context, the undeniable homogeneity in the author-text-reader configuration obtaining in thirteenth-century *clerecía* poetry has led modern critics to view the fourteenth-century departures from this norm as anomalous, imperfect and degenerate. It is, however, both unprecedented and wholly unreasonable to presuppose that either *clerecía* or, indeed, any literary *mentalité* would remain constant throughout a two-hundred year period.

In attempting to further clarify the poetic concept of *clerecía* (*clergie* in Old French), López Estrada is quite right in looking to the medieval French literary canon for clues, specifically to Brunetto Latini's usage of the Old French *cler* in the *Tresor* (c. 1265) (*"Mester de clerecía,"* pp. 169-70). From his reading of this text he concludes that: "El *Tresor* acusa los dos núcleos semánticos fundamentales, emparejando unas veces el término *cler* con él que sirve de Jesucristo a través de la Iglesia, y otras veces con él que conoce la sabiduría, el filósofo" (*"Mester de clerecía,"* p. 170).

However, perhaps more potentially illuminating than the *Tresor* is Benoît de Sainte-Maure's prologue to the *Roman de Troie*. For it is in this text (c. 1165) that clerkliness and the *translatio studii* topos to which it is inextricably linked are defined explicitly and elaborated at length. [2]

Broadly speaking, the "given" of the clerk's authority would not exist, were it not for the concept of *translatio studii et imperii*. The written word of the *translatio studii* corpus is, as the

---

[1] Francisco López Estrada, "'Mester de clerecía': Las palabras y el concepto," *Journal of Hispanic Philology*, 3 (1978), p. 165, observes: "Deyermond señala con razón que no forman un grupo los poemas juglarescos y los que están fuera de la cuaderna vía, ni los poemas de la cuaderna vía se pueden reunir en un conjunto con la suficiente homogeneidad literaria."

[2] For a well documented discussion of metrical, linguistic, demographic and geographic factors linking Spanish and French clerkly poetry, see Brian Dutton's important study, "French Influences in the Spanish *Mester de clerecía,*" *Medieval Studies in Honor of Robert White Linker*, eds. Brian Dutton, J. W. Haskell and John E. Keller (Madrid: Castalia, 1973), pp. 73-93.

clerkly poet reminds us, all that escapes the obliteration of time; it is the only possible means of sustaining the actual deeds of the *translatio imperii* (and the lessons to be gained from their contemplation), even after the "glowing ash is dead" as Chrétien says of Greece and Rome in his own lifetime. Such is the case because the *translatio studii* represents a conjoining of past-present-and-future which is recorded for two purposes. Firstly, it serves a didactic function by preserving the wisdom of the *auctores:* we must understand what is written in God's book (His creation, the world in its enduring qualities as well as its mutabilities), remembering who we are and from whom we are descended (our significance in the *continuum* of human history). Thus, since this collective memory can only be sustained by virtue of books, we arrive at the equation: Process of the world = Process of books. Because books contain that which is worthy of remembrance (as a result of its didactic nature), books themselves are inherently worthy as repositories for the wisdom of the ages.

The second justification for the dissemination of the *translatio studii* notion stems from a poetic concern, namely the need to legitimize the clerk's *remaniement* of the traditional subject matter — to dignify his own creative reading which is based on this *continuum* of learnedness (thus a self-authentification of the poet-narrator). These two components of the *translatio studii* concept are treated to substantially different ends in the *Roman de Troie* and in *Cligés*, for example, a fact which may be viewed as an illustration of the changes which the concept itself underwent in both France and Spain.

The prologue to the *Roman de Troie* outlines the all-important process of collective remembering (which is at the root of the *translatio studii* topos) quite unambiguously, and for this reason it deserves our attention in exploring the nature of *clerecía*.[3] Benoît begins his prologue by recalling the topos which claims that: "The possession of knowledge makes it one's duty to impart it" (Curtius, p. 87). And this idea is reiterated several times in the prologue.

---

[3] My treatment of the clerkly narrator figure is indebted to the work of Karl D. Uitti, esp. to "The Clerkly Narrator Figure in Old French Hagiography and Romance," *Medioevo Romanzo* 2 (1975), 394-408, and *Story, Myth and Celebration in Old French Narrative Poetry, 1050-1200* (Princeton: Princeton University Press, 1973).

Benoît follows this statement with an explanation of the rationale underlying the duty to convey one's knowledge, saying that if knowledge were not transmitted, human life would be reduced to "bestial oblivion," and people would not even be able to distinguish the sun because of their extreme ignorance (vv. 11-15). [4] "Science" which is not communicated becomes forgotten and lost forever ("obliëe et perdue," v. 20), whereas "science qu'est bien oïe / Germe e florist e fructifie" (vv. 23-24). Thus the transmission of learning carries with it a creative potential, it can bloom and bear fruit.

Next Benoît explains to his audience his own link in this essential transference of learning:

> E por ço [because this wisdom must be imparted]
>   me vueil travaillier
> En une estoire comencier,
> Que de latin, ou jo la truis,
> Si j'ai le sen e se jo puis,
> La voudrai si en romanz mettre. (vv. 33-37)

> [And for this reason I wish to begin working on a story which I found in Latin and which (if I am able) I would like to render into the vernacular.] [5]

Up to this point Benoît has expressed in an expository manner the conventional justification which the *translatio studii* offers: for itself — it being the only way to disseminate the unbroken *continuum* of wisdom which occurs in a given text; for the poet — who is performing the admirable task of communicating this knowledge in his text; and for the audience — which will profit by being able to read the text.

Yet what follows this traditional argument for the validity and dignity of *clergie* is a dramatization of the *translatio studii continuum*. The *Troie* poet tells us that Dares (an eye-witness to the events of the Trojan war) wrote down a faithful (true) account of the war — and he did so in Greek. This account was lost but later recovered by the Roman Cornelius who translated Dares'

---

[4] Benoît de Sainte-Maure. *Le Roman de Troie*. Ed. Léopold Constans. S.A.T.F. (Paris: Firmin Didot, 1904-12), vol. 1.

[5] Translation mine.

text into Latin. This second version also barely escaped passing into oblivion, yet it survived because: "Beneeiz de Saint More l'a contrové" (v. 132-33) and he, as we know, translates it into the vernacular. In this way both a geographic transference (Greece-Rome-France) as well as a linguistic transference (Greek-Latin-Romanz) have been effected. And, moreover, both are literally and simultaneously true. This series of texts dealing with the Trojan war, then, both explains and proves the process of the *translatio studii*.

A further dimension of the *translatio studii* topos operates in the *Roman de Troie* which accords to Benoît an authority more valid than that of Homer. Relying upon Dares's eye-witness account Benoît himself becomes (by extension) an eye-witness to the events which his poem treats. Homer, on the other hand, having been born one hundred years after the Trojan war, could only learn of it from second hand sources. For this reason, although he was a "clers merveillos / e sages e esciëntos ... ne dist pas sis livres veir," vv. 45-46, 51 ["an excellent poet, full of wisdom ... his book does not tell the truth"]. And while Benoît does not dispute the fact that "sis livres fu receüz / e en autorité tenuz," vv. 73-74 ["his book was received and held in high esteem"], he rejects the Homeric account in the name of "truth." Benoît thus exploits the *translatio studii* topos in order to replace the venerated Homer by himself — claiming that he is a more truthful authority for the Trojan war.

In the *Roman de Troie,* then, the *translatio studii* concept is invoked in order to celebrate clerkly "bookishness" above all — in the service of the "truth."

Turning now to a consideration of *Cligés* [6] we see that Chrétien's prologue adheres to the model of Benoît to the extent that it speaks of a continuity of texts:

> Ceste estoire trovons escrite,
> Que conter vos vuel et retraire,
> En un des livres de l'aumaire
> Mon seignor saint Pere a Biauvez;
> De la fu li contes estrez
> Qui tesmoingne l'estoire a voire:
> Por ce fet ele mialz a croire.

---

[6] My discussion of clerkliness in *Cligés*'s prologue is based on Freeman, *The Poetics of 'Translatio Studii' and 'Conjoincture'*, pp. 21-44.

> Par les livres que nos avons
> Les fez des ancïens savons
> Et del siegle qui fu jadis.
> Ce nos ont nostre livre apris
> Qu'an Grece ot de chevalerie
> Le premier los et de clergie.
> Puis vint chevalerie a Rome
> Et de la clergie la some,
> Qui or est an France venue. (vv. 18-33) [7]

[This story which I intend to relate to you, we find written in one of the books of the library of my lord St. Peter at Beauvais. From there the material was drawn on which Chrétien has made this romance. The book is very old in which the story is told, and this adds to its authority. From such books which have been preserved we learn the deeds of men of old and of the times long since gone by. Our books have informed us that the preeminence in chivalry and learning once belonged to Greece. Then chivalry passed to Rome, together with that highest learning which now has come to France.] [8]

Thus the *translatio studii* is accepted here at face value — as the means of communicating historical truth. Yet at the same time, in oblique (ironic) ways, Chrétien defies, as it were, the chivalric subject matter of the clerkly transference in order to underscore not the role of history but rather his own preeminent role as the clerkly artificer of his own creation. In other words, what we see in his text is the *translatio studii* in the service of "poetic truth."

This evocation of the traditional notion of the *translatio studii* for Chrétien's altered purpose occurs by means of various departures from the prologue canon and from the conventions of chivalry as well. For one thing, he begins the prologue by speaking of his own accomplishments in the field of literature in terms traditionally reserved for the cataloguing of knightly deeds:

> Cil qui fist d'Erec et d'Enide,
> Et les comandemanz d'Ovide
> Et l'art d'amors an romans mist,

---

[7] Chrétien de Troyes. *Cligés*. Ed. Alexandre Micha. Classiques Français du Moyen Age (Paris: Champion, 1970).
[8] Chrétien de Troyes. *Arthurian Romances* trans., W. W. Comfort (New York: Dutton, 1975), p. 91.

> Et le mors de l'espaule fist,
> Del roi Marc et d'Ysalt la blonde,
> Et de la hupe et de l'aronde
> Et del rossignol la muance,
> Un novel conte rancomance
> D'un vaslet qui en Grece fu
> Del linage le roi Artu.   (vv. 1-10)

> [He who wrote of Erec and Enide, and translated into French the commands of Ovid and the Art of Love, and wrote the *Shoulder Bite,* and about King Mark and the fair Iseut, and about the metamorphosis of the Lapwing, the Swallow, and the Nightingale, will tell another story now about a youth who lived in Greece and was a member of King Arthur's line.] (91)

By contrast, the hero's name is never mentioned in the prologue and only one of his traits — not a deed by which he had distinguished himself but rather a fact of lineage — defines him (the fact that he is King Arthur's grand-nephew). Moreover the hero, because he is part of Arthur's line, does not himself belong to the Greece-Rome-France *continuum* at all — but instead to a later, and by comparison, undistinguished, Greece. For as Chrétien admits in his prologue: "des Grezois ne des Romains / Ne dit an mes ne plus ne mains, / D'ax est la parole remese / Et estainte la vive brese." vv. 39-42 ["of Greeks and Romans no more is heard, their fame is passed and their glowing ash is dead"]. (Of course, these ancients are far from being extinct, for Chrétien rekindles the "glowing ash" of the Greek material in the very next breath with an account of the Greek Emperor and his progeny.) Nonetheless, Cligés, by virtue of his being from Greece (albeit a less illustrious land by this time) and Arthur's grand-nephew as well, exists as a literary incarnation, a living embodiment of the *translatio studii* topos. Further, considering the body of the text in light of the prologue's assertions regarding our ancestors and their ideals of *clergie,* Cligés and his father fall short of being chivalric exemplars in that their deeds are achieved through deceit, disguise and/or magic. Finally, after claiming in the prologue that *chevalrie* (as well as *clergie*) currently resides in France, none of the action of *Cligés* takes place there. (Yet the *clergie,* of course, is entirely French.)

Thus Chrétien exploits the *translatio studii* topos in order to focus our attention above all not on historical or chivalric activity, but rather on the poetic activity of the *cler* — on his creative re-elaboration of traditional material not in the service of historical "truth" (Benoît's overriding concern in the *Troie* prologue) but in the service of his own artifice. From this we see that the historical/chivalric subject matter of the *translatio studii* topos evolves from something which seems at first to be taken at face value (and whose authority is not questioned), becoming thereafter a convention to be refashioned in a creative manner (in the case of *Cligés* to underscore the artistry of the poet-narrator himself).

Yet the change which is witnessed here with respect to the poetic function of the *translatio studii* concept should be regarded as an analogue for the broader *continuum* of *translatio* as Bernard of Chartres conceived it — as the elaboration of a metaphor, a fundamental literary principle of medieval poetics and one of the four indispensable poetic resources of the *cler* according to John of Salisbury (along with *iunctura,* critical reading, and creative imitation).[9] *Translatio* in the sense of "the transferring to one word the sense of another" — the "one word unit" of a metaphor as Bernard of Chartres describes it — may also be said to function on a broader scale in the creative *translatio* of the *translatio studii* topos. For if we accept *translatio studii* as a metaphor for the clerkly activity of creative philology it too at first seems to be taken at face value later being elaborated in increasingly diversified contexts.

Just as French *clergie* represents not a static concept but a poetic process, such is also the case with the *mester de clerecía.* Clearly, medieval Spain does not envision the *translatio* as going from Greece to Rome to France, but rather from Rome to Spain. Nonetheless, the identity of the poet (his valorization of his literary refashioning of traditional subject matter), as well as the author-text-reader relationship, are essentially the same.

Virtually all of the Spanish *clerecía* texts — the *Alexander,* the *Apolonio,* nearly all the works of Berceo, *Fernán González,* the *Libro,* the *Rimado de Palacio,* etc. are inscribed prayers which rely

---

[9] John of Salisbury. *The Metalogicon* trans., Daniel D. McGarry (Gloucester: Peter Smith, 1971), esp. p. 69.

upon the authority of the written word, a written source — ultimately upon the authority of Scripture, of the world as Book. The implied audience in each case is the medieval Christian community. At the same time, however, the poet in question is a highly sophisticated manipulator of literary tradition, particularly of generic constructs. [10]

What sets Juan Ruiz apart from his predecessors is not a radical break on his part, but rather, on the one hand, an expansion of the poetic possibilities established by the *mester de clerecía* poets of the thirteenth century. His text represents continuity and development rather than anomaly. Like his predecessors, he too engages in generic experimentation and innovation, as evidenced by his remotivation of forms which are entirely traditional, as Lecoy established. Beyond this re-deployment of canonical forms, however, what constitutes Juan Ruiz's unique achievement — based on his theory of reader-response — is his recasting of the imitative discourse of the *mester de clerecía* into representational discourse.

---

[10] See in this regard my "Pagan and Christian: The Bivalent Hero of the *Libro de Alexandre*," *Kentucky Romance Quarterly*, 31 (1983), 263-70, and "Writing and Scripture in the *Libro de Apolonio*: The Conflation of Hagiography and Romance," *Hispanic Review*, 51 (1983), 159-74.

SELECTIVE BIBLIOGRAPHY

Editions

Anonymous. *The Book of Apollonius.* Trans. Raymond L. Grismer and Elizabeth Atkins. Minneapolis: University of Minnesota Press, 1936.
———. *Libro de Apolonio.* Ed. Manuel Alvar. 3 vols. Valencia: Castalia, 1977.
Augustine. *Confessions.* Ed. G. P. Gould. 2 vols. Cambridge, Mass.: Harvard University Press, 1967.
———. *Confessions.* Trans. R. S. Pine-Coffin. Hammondsworth: Penguin, 1961.
Benoît de Sainte-Maure. *Le Roman de Troie.* Ed. Léopold Constans. 6 vols. S.A.T.F. Paris: Firmin Didot, 1904-12.
Biblia sacra. Salamanca: Biblioteca de Autores Cristianos, 1965.
Chrétien de Troyes. *Cligés.* Ed. Alexandre Micha. Classiques Français du Moyen Age. Paris: Champion, 1970.
———. *Arthurian Romances.* Trans. W. W. Comfort. New York: Dutton, 1975.
Marie de France, *The 'Lais' of Marie de France.* Trans. Robert Hanning and Joan Ferrante. Durham, North Carolina: Labyrinth Press, 1978.
Martínez de Toledo, Alfonso. *Arcipreste de Talavera o Corbacho.* Ed. Joaquín González Muela. Madrid: Castalia, 1970.
Oxford Annotated Bible. Eds. Herbert G. May and Bruce M. Metzger. Oxford: Oxford University Press, 1962.
Ruiz, Juan. *Libro de buen amor.* Ed. Joan Corominas. Madrid: Gredos, 1967.
———. *Libro de buen amor.* Eds. Manuel Criado de Val and Eric W. Naylor. Madrid: C.S.I.C., 1965.
———. *Libro de buen amor.* Ed. and trans., Raymond S. Willis. Princeton: Princeton University Press, 1972.
Salisbury, John of. *The Metalogicon.* Trans., Daniel D. McGarry. Gloucester: Peter Smith, 1971.
Santillana, Marqués de. *Poesías completas.* Ed. Manuel Durán. 2 vols. Madrid: Castalia, 1980.

Secondary Works

Álvarez, Nicolás Emilio. "Análisis estructuralista del Prefacio del *Libro de buen amor,*" *Kentucky Romance Quarterly,* 28 (1981), 237-53.

Álvarez, Nicolás Emilio. "El epílogo del *Libro de buen amor.*" *Medieval, Renaissance and Folklore Studies in Honor of John Esten Keller.* Ed. Joseph R. Jones. Newark, Del.: Juan de la Cuesta, 1980, pp. 141-50.

Armistead, Samuel G. "An Unnoticed Fifteenth-Century Citation of the *Libro de buen amor.*" *Hispanic Review,* 41 (1973), 88-91.

Aubrun, Charles V. "'Buen amor': Approximations," *Homenaje a don Agapito Rey.* Ed. Josep Roca-Pons. Bloomington: Department of Spanish and Portuguese, University of Indiana, 1980, pp. 73-89.

Bandera, Cesáreo. "De la apertura del *Libro* de Juan Ruiz a Derrida y viceversa," *Dispositio,* 2 (1977), 54-66.

Booth, Wayne C. *Critical Understanding. The Powers and Limits of Pluralism.* Chicago: University of Chicago Press, 1979.

———. *A Rhetoric of Irony.* Chicago: University of Chicago Press, 1974.

Bradley, Ritamary. "Backgrounds of the Title *Speculum* in Medieval Literature." *Speculum,* 29 (1954), 100-15.

Brownlee, Marina Scordilis. "Autobiography as Self-(Re)Presentation: The Augustinian Paradigm and Juan Ruiz's Theory of Reading." *Mimesis: From Mirror to Method.* Eds. John D. Lyons and Stephen G. Nichols. Hanover and London: University Press of New England, 1982, pp. 71-82.

———. "Pagan and Christian: The Bivalent Hero of the *Libro de Alexandre.*" *Kentucky Romance Quarterly,* 31 (1983), 263-70.

———. "Permutations of the Narrator-Protagonist Configuration: The *Serrana* Episodes of the *Libro de buen amor* in Light of the Doña Endrina Sequence." *Romance Notes,* 22 (1981), 98-101.

———. "Writing and Scripture in the *Libro de Apolonio:* The Conflation of Hagiography and Romance." *Hispanic Review,* 51 (1983), 159-74.

Burke, James F. "Love's Double Cross: Language Play as Structure in the *Libro de buen amor.*" *University of Toronto Quarterly,* 43 (1974), 231-62.

———. "Juan Ruiz, the *Serranas* and the Rites of Spring." *Journal of Medieval and Renaissance Studies,* 5 (1975), 13-35.

Caba, Rubén. *Por la ruta serrana del Arcipreste.* Madrid: Cenit, 1977.

Castro, Américo. "El *Libro de buen amor* del Arcipreste de Hita." *Comparative Literature,* 4 (1952), 193-213.

———. *The Structure of Spanish History.* Trans. Edmund L. King. Princeton: Princeton University Press, 1954.

Catalán, Diego, with Suzy Petersen. "'Aunque omne non goste la pera del peral...' (Sobre la 'sentencia' de Juan Ruiz y la de su buen amor)." *Hispanic Review,* 38, No. 5 (1970), 56-96.

Chapman, Janet A. "Juan Ruiz's Learned Sermon." *"Libro de buen amor" Studies* Ed. G. B. Gybbon-Monypenny. London: Tamesis, 1970, pp. 29-52.

Colish, Marcia L. *The Mirror of Language: A Study in the Medieval Theory of Knowledge.* New Haven: Yale University Press, 1968.

Curtius, Ernst Robert. *European Literature and the Latin Middle Ages.* Trans. Willard R. Trask. Princeton: Princeton University Press, 1953.

Dal, Erik. *The Ages of Man and the Months of the Year: Poetry, Prose and Pictures Outlining the 'Douze Mois Figurées' Motif Found in Shepherds Calendars and in 'Livres d'Heures' (14th to 17th Century).* Copenhagen: Munksgaard, 1980.

Deyermond, Alan D. "The Greeks, the Romans, the Astrologers and the Meaning of the *Libro de buen amor.*" *Romance Notes,* 5 (1963), 88-91.

Deyermond, Alan D. "Juan Ruiz's Attitude to Literature." *Medieval, Renaissance and Folklore Studies in Honor of John Esten Keller*. Ed. Joseph R. Jones. Newark: Juan de la Cuesta, 1980, pp. 113-25.
———. "'Mester es sen pecado.'" *Romanische Forschungen*, 77 (1965), 111-16.
———. "Some Aspects of Parody in the *Libro de buen amor*." *'Libro de buen amor' Studies*. Ed. G. B. Gybbon-Monypenny. London: Tamesis, 1970, pp. 53-78.
Dutton, Brian. "*Buen amor:* Its Meaning and Uses in Some Medieval Texts." *'Libro de buen amor' Studies*. Ed. G. B. Gybbon-Monypenny. London: Tamesis, 1970, pp. 95-121.
———. "'Con Dios en Buen Amor': A Semantic Analysis of the Title of the *Libro de buen amor*." *Bulletin of Hispanic Studies*, 43 (1966), 161-76.
———. "French Influences in the Spanish *Mester de clerecía*." *Medieval Studies in Honor of Robert White Linker*. Eds. Brian Dutton, J. W. Haskell and John E. Keller. Madrid: Castalia, 1973, pp. 73-93.
Ferraresi, Alicia C. de. *De amor y poesía en la España medieval: prólogo a Juan Ruiz*. México, D. F.: Colegio de México, 1976.
Forastieri Braschi, Eduardo. "La descripción de los meses en el *Libro de buen amor*." *Revista de Filología Española*, 55 (1972), 213-32.
Foulet, Alfred and Uitti, Karl D. "The Prologue to the *Lais* of Marie de France: A Reconsideration." *Romance Philology*, 35 (1982), 242-49.
Freccero, John. "The Fig Tree and the Laurel: Petrarch's Poetics." *Diacritics*, 5 (1975), 34-40.
Freeman, Michelle A. *The Poetics of 'Translatio Studii' and 'Conjoincture': Chrétien de Troyes's 'Cligés'*. Lexington: French Forum, 1979.
Frye, Northrop. *The Secular Scripture*. Cambridge: Harvard University Press, 1978.
Gerli, E. Michael. "'Recta voluntas est bonus amor': St. Augustine and the Didactic Structure of the *Libro de buen amor*," *Romance Philology*, 35 (1982), 500-508.
Gilman, Stephen. "The Death of Lazarillo de Tormes," *PMLA*, 81 (1966), 149-66.
Gumbrecht, Hans Ulrich. "Aspectos de una historia recepcional del *Libro de buen amor*." *Cuadernos Hispanoamericanos*, 282 (1972-73), 598-610.
Gybbon-Monypenny, G. B. "Autobiography in the *Libro de buen amor* in the Light of Some Literary Comparisons." *Bulletin of Hispanic Studies*, 34 (1957), 63-78.
———. "The Spanish *Mester de Clerecía* and Its Intended Public: Concerning the Validity as Evidence of Passages of Direct Address to the Audience." *Medieval Miscellany Presented to Eugène Vinaver*. Eds. Frederick Whitehead, A. H. Diverres and F. E. Sutcliffe. Manchester: Manchester University Press, 1965, pp. 230-44.
———. "The Two Versions of the *Libro de buen amor:* The Extent and Nature of the Author's Revision." *Bulletin of Hispanic Studies*, 39 (1962), 205-21.
Hamilton, Rita. "The Digression on Confession in the *Libro de buen amor*." *'Libro de buen amor' Studies*. Ed. G. B. Gybbon-Monypenny. London: Tamesis, 1970, pp. 149-57.
Hart, Thomas R. *La alegoría en el 'Libro de buen amor'*. Madrid: Revista de Occidente, 1959.

Hirsch, E. D. *Validity in Interpretation*. Chicago: University of Chicago Press, 1967.
Iser, Wolfgang. *The Act of Reading*. Baltimore: Johns Hopkins University Press, 1978.
Jauss, Hans-Robert. "Littérature médiévale et théorie des genres." *Poétique*, 1 (1970), 79-101.
Kellermann, Wilhelm. "Zur Charakteristik des *Libro de buen amor del Arcipreste de Hita*." *Zeitschrift für romanische Philologie*, 67 (1951), 225-54.
Kinkade, Richard P. "'Intellectum tibi dabo...': The Function of Free Will in the *Libro de buen amor*." *Bulletin of Hispanic Studies*, 47 (1970), 296-315.
Lecoy, Félix. *Recherches sur le 'Libro de buen amor' de Juan Ruiz*. Reprinted with a new Prologue, Supplementary Bibliography and Index by A. D. Deyermond. Farnborough, Hants: Gregg International, 1974.
Lida de Malkiel, María Rosa. "Nuevas Notas para la interpretación del *Libro de buen amor*." *Nueva Revista de Filología Hispánica*, 13 (1959), 17-82.
―――. "Thomas R. Hart. *La alegoría en el 'Libro de buen amor.'*" *Romance Philology*, 14 (1961), 340-43.
―――. *Two Spanish Masterpieces: The 'Book of Good Love' and 'The Celestina.'* Illinois Studies in Language and Literature, 49. Urbana: University of Illinois Press, 1961.
López Estrada, Francisco. "'Mester de clerecía': La palabra y el concepto." *Journal of Hispanic Philology*, 3 (1978), 165-74.
Menéndez Pidal, Ramón. *Poesía juglaresca y orígenes de las literaturas románicas*. 6th ed. Madrid: Instituto de Estudios Políticos. 1957.
Michael, Ian. "The Function of the Popular Tale in the *Libro de buen amor*." *'Libro de buen amor' Studies*. Ed. G. B. Gybbon-Monypenny. London: Tamesis, 1970, pp. 177-219.
Michalski, André. "La parodia hagiográfica y el dualismo eros-thanatos en el *Libro de buen amor*." *Actas del I Congreso Internacional sobre el Arcipreste de Hita*. Ed. Manuel Criado de Val. Barcelona: S.E.R.E.S.A., 1973, pp. 57-77.
Moffatt, Lucius G. "The Evidence of Early Mentions of the Archpriest of Hita or of His Work." *MLN*, 75 (1960), 33-40.
Myers, Oliver T. "Symmetry of Form in the *Libro de buen amor*." *Philological Quarterly*, 51 (1972), 74-84.
Nepaulsingh, Colbert. "The Rhetorical Structure of the Prologues to the *Libro de buen amor* and the *Celestina*." *Bulletin of Hispanic Studies*, 51 (1974), 325-34.
―――. "The Structure of the *Libro de buen amor*." *Neophilologus*, 61 (1977), 53-73.
Ong, Walter. "The Writer's Audience is Always a Fiction." *PMLA*, 90 (1975), 9-21.
Parker, Alexander A. "Thomas R. Hart, *La alegoría en el 'Libro de buen amor.'* Madrid: Revista de Occidente, 1959." *MLN*, 77 (1962), 558-59.
Phillips, Gail. *The Imagery of the 'Libro de buen amor'*. Madison: Hispanic Seminary of Medieval Studies, 1983.
Rand, E. K. "Editor's Preface." *Speculum*, 1 (1926), 4.
Read, M. K. "Man Against Language: A Linguistic Perspective on the Theme of Alienation in the *Libro de buen amor*," *MLN*, 96 (1981), 237-60.

Rico, Francisco. "Sobre el origen de la autobiografía en el *Libro de buen amor.*" *Anuario de Estudios Medievales,* 4 (1967), 301-25.
Seidenspinner-Núñez, Dayle. *The Allegory of Good Love: Parodic Perspectivism in the 'Libro de buen amor.'* Berkeley: University of California Press, 1981.
Spitzer, Leo. *Classical and Christian Ideas of World Harmony.* Baltimore: Johns Hopkins University Press, 1963.
———. "Note on the Poetic and the Empirical 'I' in Medieval Authors." *Traditio,* 4 (1946), 414-22.
———. "En torno al arte del Arcipreste de Hita." *Lingüística e historia literaria.* Madrid: Gredos, 1955, pp. 103-60.
Sturm, Sara. "The Greeks and the Romans: The Archpriest's Warning to his Reader." *Romance Notes,* 10 (1968-69), 404-12.
Tate, R. B. "Adventures in the Sierra." *'Libro de buen amor' Studies.* Ed. G. B. Gybbon-Monypenny. Tamesis, 1970, pp. 219-29.
Todorov, Tzvetan. "Reading as Construction." *The Reader in the Text.* Eds. Susan R. Sulieman and Inge Crossman. Princeton: Princeton University Press, 1980, pp. 67-82.
Uitti, Karl D. "The Clerkly Narrator Figure in Old French Hagiography and Romance." *Medioevo Romanzo,* 2 (1975), 394-408.
———. *Story, Myth and Celebration in Old French Narrative Poetry, 1050-1200.* Princeton: Princeton University Press, 1973.
Ullman, Pierre L. "Juan Ruiz's Prologue." *MLN,* 82 (1967), 149-70.
———. "Stanzas 140-150 of the *Libro de buen amor.*" *PMLA,* 79 (1964), 200-05.
Vance, Eugene. "Augustine's *Confessions* and the Grammar of Selfhood." *Genre,* 4 (1973), 1-28.
———. "Augustine's *Confessions* and the Poetics of the Law." *MLN,* 98 (1978), 618-34.
———. "Le moi comme langage: Saint Augustin et l'autobiographie." *Poétique,* 14 (1973), 163-78.
Vetterling, Mary-Anne. "The Rediscovery of the *Libro de buen amor.*" *Dieciocho,* 4 (1981), 24-33.
Walker, Roger M. "Juan Ruiz's Defense of Love." *MLN,* 89 (1969), 292-97.
———. "Towards an Interpretation of the *Libro de buen amor.*" *Bulletin of Hispanic Studies,* 43 (1966), 1-10.
Walsh, John K. "Juan Ruiz and the *mester de clerecía.* Lost Context and Lost Parody in the *Libro de buen amor.*" *Romance Philology,* 33 (1979), 62-86.
Wardropper, Bruce W. "Pleberio's Lament for Melibea and the Medieval Elegiac Tradition." *MLN* (1964), 140-52.
Webster, James C. *The Labors of the Months in Antique and Medieval Art.* Princeton: Princeton University Press, 1938.
Willis, Raymond S. "'Mester de Clerecía': A Definition of the *Libro de Alexandre.*" *Romance Philology,* 10 (1957), 212-24.
———. "Two Trotaconventos." *Romance Philology,* 17 (1963), 353-62.
Zahareas, Anthony N. *The Art of Juan Ruiz Archpriest of Hita.* Madrid: Estudios de Literatura Española, 1965.
———. "The Stars: Worldly Love and Free Will in the *Libro de buen amor.*" *Bulletin of Hispanic Studies,* 42 (1965), 82-93.

Zahareas, Anthony N. "Structure and Ideology in the *Libro de buen amor*." *La Corónica*, 7 (1979), 92-104.

Zink, Michel. *La Pastourelle. Poésie et folklore au moyen-âge*. Paris: Bordas, 1972.

INDEX

Aeneid: 117
Álvarez, Nicolás Emilio: 25 n., 52n., 120n.
Arcipreste de Talavera: 13
Armistead, Samuel G.: 14n.
ars amatoria: 14, 21, 91
ars poetica: 21, 51
astrology: 77-80
Atkins, Elizabeth: 37n.
Aubrun, Charles: 100n.
Augustine
   Confessions: 17, 23, 25-26, 28-35, 36-46, 49, 55, 59, 66-68, 77, 78, 88, 105, 106-07, 109, 116-19
   De doctrina christiana: 29n.
   De magistro: 29n.
   De trinitate: 25
autobiography: 16, 17, 18, 19, 46n., 54, 55, 56, 58, 111, 112, 113-14, 118

Bandera, Cesáreo: 15
Benoît de Sainte-Maure: 123-26, 129
Berceo, Gonzalo de: 37n., 53n., 94, 129
bildungsroman: 59
Boccaccio, Giovanni: 11, 102
Bonaventure: 106
Booth, Wayne C.: 19, 98, 99-101, 103-04
Bradley, Ritamary: 108-09
Breviloquium: 106
Brownlee, Marina Scordilis: 58n., 129n.
Brunetto Latini: 123
Burke, James F.: 57n., 70n.

Caba, Rubén: 57n.

Caballero Zifar: 78
cancionero: 14, 16, 114, 119
Capellanus, Andreas: 102
Castro, Américo: 16, 17, 53, 111, 112, 113
Catalán, Diego: 12n., 49
Chapman, Janet A.: 26n.
Chartres, Bernard of: 129
Chaucer, Geoffrey: 102
Chrétien de Troyes: 124, 126-29
Cligés: 124, 126-29
Colish, Marcia L.: 33, 88, 117-18
El collar de la paloma (The Dove's Neckring): 17
El conde Lucanor: 94
cuaderna vía: 16n., 122
Curtius, Ernst Robert: 52n., 105-06, 124

Dal, Erik: 70n.-71n.
De vetula: 113-14
Deyermond, Alan D.: 14n., 65n., 73n., 75, 77, 116
Dutton, Brian: 13n., 100n., 123n.

exemplum: 17, 19, 67, 74, 76, 77, 80, 88-97, 102, 109, 120
exsuperatio: 72, 73

fabula: 118
Fernán González: 129
fig tree: 32, 40, 55
Forastieri Braschi, Eduardo: 71n.
Foulet, Alfred: 20 n.
Freccero, John: 32-33, 41, 43
Freeman, Michelle: 55n., 126n.
Frye, Northrop: 38n.-39n.

Gerli, E. Michael: 29n.
Gilman, Stephen: 73n.
Green, Otis H.: 78
Grismer, Raymond L.: 37n.
Gumbrecht, Hans Ulrich: 22n.
Gybbon-Monypenny, G. B.: 13n., 18, 24, 38n., 56n., 111, 114

hagiography: 17, 59, 114, 122, 130n.
Hamilton, Rita: 84-85
Hart, Thomas: 52n., 53n., 102, 103
Hirsch, E. D.: 111
historia: 118
Homer: 126
Hugh of St. Victor: 103

Ibn Hazm: 17
imitation (imitative texts): 32, 45, 53, 55, 109, 130
implied reader: 13, 43, 73, 99, 102
inscribed reader: 12, 13, 43, 49
Iser, Wolfgang: 11, 13n., 19

Jauss, Hans-Robert: 13, 115n.
juglar: 18, 19, 56, 111

Kellermann, Wilhelm: 54n.
Kinkade, Richard P.: 24, 26-28

Lais: 20
Lazarillo de Tormes: 73n.
Lecoy, Félix: 14, 15, 17, 24, 25, 85, 111, 112, 118, 130
Libro de Alexandre: 37n., 129
Libro de Apolonio: 37n., 91, 129
Libro de buen amor
  Astrologers: 74, 75n., 76-78
  Death: 62, 68
  Devil: 17, 60, 64, 69, 72, 82, 94, 95
  Don Amor: 57, 59, 60-61, 64, 67, 69, 70, 72, 79, 80, 83n., 87, 89, 90, 91-93, 96, 98, 100, 101, 114, 116
  Don Carnal: 14, 69, 73, 79, 84-87, 93, 98, 112
  Don Melón: 55, 56
  Doña Cuaresma: 14, 69, 73, 84, 98, 100, 101, 112
  Doña Endrina: 14, 55-57, 67, 89, 92, 93, 112, 116
  Doña Garoça: 60, 80-81, 83, 89, 92, 93, 94, 95, 116
  Doña Venus: 67, 79-80
  Greeks and Romans: 74-75, 76, 104
  Money: 92
  Moorish Girl: 82, 83
  Pitas Payas: 89-90
  serranas: 56-58, 67, 115
  Trotaconventos: 56, 60, 61-62, 65, 66, 67, 68, 78, 82, 89, 92, 93, 94, 100, 116
  Virgin Mary: 60, 61, 64, 65, 67, 71, 101n., 115
Lida de Malkiel, María Rosa: 16n., 17, 52n., 53n., 54n., 75, 84, 89, 103, 111, 113
López Estrada, Francisco: 123

Manuel, Don Juan: 53n., 94
maqamat: 17, 103, 113
Marie de France: 20, 21
Marqués de Santillana: 13
Mc Grady, Donald: 90n.
memory: 29-31, 39-42, 43n., 44, 46-48, 49, 53, 66, 69, 105
Menéndez Pelayo, Marcelino: 123
Menéndez Pidal, Ramón: 16, 24, 111, 112
mester de clerecía: 12, 16n., 18, 19, 37, 122-30
Metalogicon: 129n.
Michael, Ian: 89, 90, 91, 94, 96
Michalski, André: 17, 59, 60, 65, 66, 67, 111, 114
midpoint: 45, 54-57, 67
Milagro de Teófilo: 94
Moffatt, Lucius G.: 14n., 33n.
Monica: 39, 65-67
Myers, Olver T.: 15

Nepaulsingh, Colbert: 15, 17, 24, 28, 59, 71-73, 111, 113, 114

Ong, Walter: 12, 18
Ovid: 92, 111, 113-14, 116, 127-28

Parker, Alexander A.: 103, 104
parody: 13n., 17, 18, 25, 29n., 52n., 57, 59, 61, 64, 65, 67, 72, 73, 78, 84

INDEX

pear tree: 30-33, 70
Petersen, Suzy (see Diego Catalán)
Phillips, Gail: 61n.
planctus: 60, 62, 64, 67-68, 79
Prudentius: 106

Rabanus Maurus: 103
Rand, E. K.: 108
Read, M. K.: 15
representation (representational texts): 32, 45, 55, 109, 130
Rico, Francisco: 111, 113-14
Rimado de palacio: 129
risala: 17, 113
romance: 38, 39n., 54, 55, 71, 122, 126, 130n.
Roman de Troie: 123-26, 129

Salisbury, John of: 129n.
Seidenspinner-Núñez, Dayle: 29n.
speculum: 105-10, 114
Spitzer, Leo: 15n., 16, 19, 20, 52, 53, 75, 111
Sturm, Sara: 75n.

Tate, R. B.: 58n.
Todorov, Tzvetan: 22
translatio studii: 55n., 123-29
Trésor: 123

Uitti, Karl D.: 20n., 124n.
Ullman, Pierre: 24-26, 28, 78

Vance, Eugene: 43, 46n., 107n.
Vetterling, Mary-Anne: 14n.
Virgil: 89, 91, 117n.

Walker, Roger M.: 15, 77, 78
Walsh, John K.: 13n., 16n.
Wardropper, Bruce W.: 61, 62n., 64n.
Webster, James C.: 70n.
Willis, R. S.: 12n., 56n., 78, 114, 116n.

Zahareas, Anthony N.: 15, 16n., 25, 26, 52n., 64n., 74, 75, 77, 78, 84, 90, 98, 99, 102, 103, 111, 112, 115, 120
Zink, Michel: 57n.

NORTH CAROLINA STUDIES IN THE ROMANCE LANGUAGES AND LITERATURES

I.S.B.N. Prefix 0-8078-

Recent Titles

A QUANTITATIVE AND COMPARATIVE STUDY OF THE VOCALISM OF THE LATIN INSCRIPTIONS OF NORTH AFRICA, BRITAIN, DALMATIA, AND THE BALKANS, by Stephen William Omeltchenko. 1977. (No. 180). -9180-0.

OCTAVIEN DE SAINT-GELAIS "LE SEJOUR D'HONNEUR", edited by Joseph A. James. 1977. (No. 181). -9181-9.

A STUDY OF NOMINAL INFLECTION IN LATIN INSCRIPTIONS, by Paul A. Gaeng. 1977. (No. 182). -9182-7.

THE LIFE AND WORKS OF LUIS CARLOS LÓPEZ, by Martha S. Bazik. 1977. (No. 183). -9183-5.

"THE CORT D'AMOR". A THIRTEENTH-CENTURY ALLEGORICAL ART OF LOVE, by Lowanne E. Jones. 1977. (No. 185). -9185-1.

PHYTONYMIC DERIVATIONAL SYSTEMS IN THE ROMANCE LANGUAGES: STUDIES IN THEIR ORIGIN AND DEVELOPMENT, by Walter E. Geiger. 1978. (No. 187). -9187-8.

LANGUAGE IN GIOVANNI VERGA'S EARLY NOVELS, by Nicholas Patruno. 1977. (No. 188). -9188-6.

BLAS DE OTERO EN SU POESÍA, by Moraima de Semprún Donahue. 1977. (No. 189). -9189-4.

LA ANATOMÍA DE "EL DIABLO COJUELO": DESLINDES DEL GÉNERO ANATOMÍSTICO, por C. George Peale. 1977. (No. 191). -9191-6.

RICHARD SANS PEUR, EDITED FROM "LE ROMANT DE RICHART" AND FROM GILLES CORROZET'S "RICHART SANS PAOUR", by Denis Joseph Conlon. 1977. (No. 192). -9192-4.

MARCEL PROUST'S GRASSET PROOFS. *Commentary and Variants*, by Douglas Alden. 1978. (No. 193). -9193-2.

MONTAIGNE AND FEMINISM, by Cecile Insdorf. 1977. (No. 194). -9194-0.

SANTIAGO F. PUGLIA, AN EARLY PHILADELPHIA PROPAGANDIST FOR SPANISH AMERICAN INDEPENDENCE, by Merle S. Simmons. 1977. (No. 195). -9195-9.

BAROQUE FICTION-MAKING. A STUDY OF GOMBERVILLE'S "POLEXANDRE", by Edward Baron Turk. 1978. (No. 196). -9196-7.

THE TRAGIC FALL: DON ÁLVARO DE LUNA AND OTHER FAVORITES IN SPANISH GOLDEN AGE DRAMA, by Raymond R. MacCurdy. 1978. (No. 197). -9197-5.

A BAHIAN HERITAGE. An Ethnolinguistic Study of African Influences on Bahian Portuguese, by William W. Megenney. 1978. (No. 198). -9198-3.

"LA QUERELLE DE LA ROSE": Letters and Documents, by Joseph L. Baird and John R. Kane. 1978. (No. 199). -9199-1.

TWO AGAINST TIME. *A Study of the Very Present Worlds of Paul Claudel and Charles Péguy*, by Joy Nachod Humes. 1978. (No. 200). -9200-9.

TECHNIQUES OF IRONY IN ANATOLE FRANCE. Essay on *Les Sept Femmes de la Barbe-Bleue*, by Diane Wolfe Levy. 1978. (No. 201). -9201-7.

THE PERIPHRASTIC FUTURES FORMED BY THE ROMANCE REFLEXES OF "VADO (AD)" PLUS INFINITIVE, by James Joseph Champion. 1978. (No. 202). -9202-5.

THE EVOLUTION OF THE LATIN /b/-/ṷ/ MERGER: A Quantitative and Comparative Analysis of the *B-V* Alternation in Latin Inscriptions, by Joseph Louis Barbarino. 1978. (No. 203). -9203-3.

METAPHORIC NARRATION: THE STRUCTURE AND FUNCTION OF METAPHORS IN "A LA RECHERCHE DU TEMPS PERDU", by Inge Karalus Crosman. 1978. (No. 204). -9204-1.

When ordering please cite the *ISBN Prefix* plus the last four digits for each title.

Send orders to: University of North Carolina Press
Chapel Hill
North Carolina 27514
U. S. A.

NORTH CAROLINA STUDIES IN THE ROMANCE LANGUAGES AND LITERATURES

I.S.B.N. Prefix 0-88438

Recent Titles

LE VAIN SIECLE GUERPIR. A Literary Approach to Sainthood through Old French Hagiography of the Twelfth Century, by Phyllis Johnson and Brigitte Cazelles. 1979. (No. 205). *-9205-X.*
THE POETRY OF CHANGE: A STUDY OF THE SURREALIST WORKS OF BENJAMIN PÉRET, by Julia Field Costich. 1979. (No. 206). *-9206-8.*
NARRATIVE PERSPECTIVE IN THE POST-CIVIL WAR NOVELS OF FRANCISCO AYALA "MUERTES DE PERRO" AND "EL FONDO DEL VASO", by Maryellen Bieder. 1979. (No. 207). *-9207-6.*
RABELAIS: HOMO LOGOS, by Alice Fiola Berry. 1979. (No. 208). *-9208-4.*
"DUEÑAS" AND "DONCELLAS": A STUDY OF THE "DOÑA RODRÍGUEZ" EPISODE IN "DON QUIJOTE", by Conchita Herdman Marianella. 1979. (No. 209). *-9209-2.*
PIERRE BOAISTUAU'S "HISTOIRES TRAGIQUES": A STUDY OF NARRATIVE FORM AND TRAGIC VISION, by Richard A. Carr. 1979. (No. 210). *-9210-6.*
REALITY AND EXPRESSION IN THE POETRY OF CARLOS PELLICER, by George Melnykovich. 1979. (No. 211). *-9211-4.*
MEDIEVAL MAN, HIS UNDERSTANDING OF HIMSELF, HIS SOCIETY, AND THE WORLD, by Urban T. Holmes, Jr. 1980. (No. 212). *-9212-2.*
MÉMOIRES SUR LA LIBRAIRIE ET SUR LA LIBERTÉ DE LA PRESSE, introduction and notes by Graham E. Rodmell. 1979. (No. 213). *-9213-0.*
THE FICTIONS OF THE SELF. THE EARLY WORKS OF MAURICE BARRES, by Gordon Shenton. 1979. (No. 214). *-9214-9.*
CECCO ANGIOLIERI. A STUDY, by Gifford P. Orwen. 1979. (No. 215). *-9215-7.*
THE INSTRUCTIONS OF SAINT LOUIS: A CRITICAL TEXT, by David O'Connell. 1979. (No. 216). *-9216-5.*
ARTFUL ELOQUENCE, JEAN LEMAIRE DE BELGES AND THE RHETORICAL TRADITION, by Michael F. O. Jenkins. 1980. (No. 217). *-9217-3.*
A CONCORDANCE TO MARIVAUX'S COMEDIES IN PROSE, edited by Donald C. Spinelli. 1979. (No. 218). 4 volumes, *-9218-1* (set); *-9219-X* (v. 1); *-9220-3* (v. 2); *-9221-1* (v. 3); *-9222-X* (v. 4.)
ABYSMAL GAMES IN THE NOVELS OF SAMUEL BECKETT, by Angela B. Moorjani. 1982. (No. 219). *-9223-8.*
GERMAIN NOUVEAU DIT HUMILIS: ÉTUDE BIOGRAPHIQUE, par Alexandre L. Amprimoz. 1983. (No. 220). *-9224-6.*
THE "VIE DE SAINT ALEXIS" IN THE TWELFTH AND THIRTEENTH CENTURIES: AN EDITION AND COMMENTARY, by Alison Goddard Elliot. 1983. (No. 221). *-9225-4.*
THE BROKEN ANGEL: MYTH AND METHOD IN VALÉRY, by Ursula Franklin. 1984. (No. 222). *-9226-2.*
READING VOLTAIRE'S "CONTES": A SEMIOTICS OF PHILOSOPHICAL NARRATION, by Carol Sherman. 1985. (No. 223). *-9227-0.*
THE STATUS OF THE READING SUBJECT IN THE "LIBRO DE BUEN AMOR", by Marina Scordilis Brownlee. 1985. (No. 224). *-9228-9.*
MARTORELL'S "TIRANT LO BLANCH": A PROGRAM FOR MILITARY AND SOCIAL REFORM IN FIFTEENTH-CENTURY CHRISTENDOM, by Edward T. Aylward. 1985. (No. 225). *-9229-7.*

When ordering please cite the *ISBN Prefix* plus the last four digits for each title.

Send orders to: University of North Carolina Press
Chapel Hill
North Carolina 27514
U. S. A.

The Department of Romance Studies Digital Arts and Collaboration Lab at the University of North Carolina at Chapel Hill is proud to support the digitization of the North Carolina Studies in the Romance Languages and Literatures series.

DEPARTMENT OF Romance Studies

Digital Arts and Collaboration Lab

www.ingramcontent.com/pod-product-compliance
Lightning Source LLC
Chambersburg PA
CBHW020419230426
43663CB00007BA/1228